HELOISE has become a phenomenon of the newspaper field. This fact is readily attested to by the *Honolulu Advertiser*, the paper that gave her a start. Its circulation jumped from about 46,000 to 71,000 in less than three years after Heloise began her famous column. Now, over 400 newspapers in the United States and Canada carry her timely advice. Heloise practices what she preaches, for most of these hints come from her own trial-and-error experiments; others have been contributed by the growing host of readers of her King Features syndicated column. Heloise and her husband, Lt. Col. Marshall Cruse, with their two children, now live near Washington, D.C.

───────────────────────

HELOISE'S
HOUSEKEEPING HINTS was originally published by Prentice-Hall, Inc.

Heloise's
HOUSEKEEPING
HINTS

by

Heloise

ILLUSTRATED

PUBLISHED BY POCKET BOOKS, INC. NEW YORK

HELOISE'S HOUSEKEEPING HINTS

Prentice-Hall edition published November, 1962

A *Pocket Book* edition

1st printing.........January, 1965
9th printing...........June, 1965

This *Pocket Book* edition includes every word
contained in the original, higher-priced edition. It is printed
from brand-new plates made from completely reset, clear, easy-to-read
type. *Pocket Book* editions are published by Pocket Books, Inc., and
are printed and distributed in the U.S.A. by Affiliated Publishers, a
division of Pocket Books, Inc., 630 Fifth Avenue, New York, N.Y. 10020.
Trademark of Pocket Books, Inc., 630 Fifth Avenue,
New York, N.Y. 10020, registered in the United States
and other countries.

L

Contents

Heloise's Housekeeping Hints

Dear Fellow Housewives

To each and every one of you mothers, housewives, homemakers everywhere, a special blessing. You most certainly deserve it!

I'm not talking here to the fanatical housekeeper (I used to be one before I took some hints!) but to the everyday housewife with children, tired working mothers, office girls and those others who just never find the time to get everything done that needs to be done. You never will . . . don't think you can.

All women have more than they can do because they take on more than they have strength for. A woman did not (in the old days) paint her kitchen, wash the car, drive the children to school, weed the lawn, pay the bills, worry about budgeting and insurance. Her husband did these things or hired someone.

Today's woman is expected to be well-read, faultlessly groomed, a nursemaid, chauffeur, laundress, seamstress, hostess, cook, gardener, painter, appliance repairman, wallpaperhanger, carpenter, exterminator (for those awful bugs of all sorts) and Jane-of-all-trades!

Being a homemaker is a big job for anyone, and you and I are going to make mistakes. But so what? That's the way we learn!

So, relieve your mind of a lot of its frustrations by simply accepting the fact that you are a woman. Next, make yourself believe that you do the best you can. Probably you do! Tranquilizers are expensive . . . so are doctors' bills. Instead of worrying yourself into a state of jitters over keeping a "perfect" house, let this book show you how to make it easier for yourself.

I'll try to write and talk in everyday simple down-to-earth language . . . as in a telephone conversation or while sharing housewives' chores with a friend and neighbor. I am no authority and I admit it! I have had to do things the hard way, by trial and experience. I am no writer and never intend to be. I am just a mother and housewife, like you. But the things in this book worked for me—they will for you too!

First of all, when your neighbor or friend tells you she has everything done . . . don't you believe it! She hasn't. No woman ever does. And won't even when she is six feet under. (That "six-feet-under" means dirt!)

Accept this fact. Don't try to keep up with your neighbor. Enjoy living day by day (and keep up with *yourself*) by learning the short cuts. Top-clean *first*, then get around to deep cleaning.

The chapters in this book are definitely concerned with "top-cleaning" and quickie-jet-age-make-do methods to help you run your home as best you can and still keep calm. (*This is your* most important job . . . keeping calm!) My main purpose is to help you get your home in order so that you may have the extra time and inclination to really deep-clean later. With your home top-cleaned and in order you will find the time to plan occasional, thorough cleaning.

Keep in mind when reading each chapter that this book was not written for anyone except *you:* my fellow woman and, I hope, my friend. Not your neighbor, not your husband, not your mother-in-law or the boss's wife. These are the very people you are trying to impress with your neatness. Keep that secret to yourself!

Keep in mind, too . . . the second wife *always* has a maid! Your husband will not look under the bed or on the ceiling at night to see if he can find a cobweb. Your husband wants a neat house and a happy wife and family. That's all!

And you know what? I have never had a guest in my home move my sofa or open a drawer to check and see if I had clutter, dirt or cobwebs! Really!

And girls, another thing. Jar loose once in a while and spend a few nickels or dollars on yourself. Don't do without those few simple things that would make your life easier, such as a carpet-sweeper, plumber's-friend, feather-duster and pants-stretchers. Spend that few dollars for them.

Life is so very short and so sweet. Live every day. Be neat and get rid of clutter and top-clean your house. It's easy! I am forty-two years old and had to learn the hard way. Take it from me: learn the short cuts.

Then spend the energy and time you have saved being kind to your family and friends, but most of all to yourself. *You* deserve it the most!

Heloise

1.

Kitchen Corner

~~~~~~

CURB YOUR APPETITE TO CURB YOUR PURSE!

To be surer of saving on grocery bills, *never* go to the market hungry! Always shop immediately after breakfast or lunch. With your stomach filled, you will not be nearly so tempted to buy condiments, luxury items and fancy foodstuffs! When hungry, you go for fancy foodstuffs to "tide you over" until dinner. If you aren't hungry, and especially if you "just can't eat another bite," they don't even tempt you! It's all psychological, but it works as a money stretcher, instead of a tummy stretcher.

Never worry about the necessities. Everybody must pay rent, taxes and buy necessary foods. Accept the fact that you cannot escape these costs. Save your "worry time" for the things you buy and don't need!

We all know we need milk, flour, sugar, eggs and potatoes! Even coffee or tea. But we can do without the fancy things. The "splurges" are what run up our grocery bills. I have had my husband say, "This is the best ham! Why don't we have it more often? How much did it cost?"

I always answer, "Just enjoy it, dear. When you finish eating, I'll tell you." Then I laugh to myself. No husband understands that ham costs more than hamburger! I know we can't afford center cut slices of ham too often. But monotony is what gets the housewife down. Don't let it at the table. Go buy that slice of ham once a month. We need to splurge once in a while. Enjoy it when you do. And . . . never feel guilty when you eat it.

Why should you? Your husband won't feel guilty. He will leave the table, his tummy will be full, he will read his paper or watch TV. *You* will be doing dishes. Think about that wonderful slice of ham then. It helps! And remember, that

5

slice of ham will cost less than all the fancy foodstuffs you might have bought if you had been hungry when you went to the market.

Save this way: Serve the ham with rice or grits, ham gravy (made with water and so less fattening) and a salad. Serve a gelatin dessert to make up for the extra pennies you spent on the ham.

If you *need* something . . . buy it. If it is not necessary . . . then check the price. But never upset yourself over things you can do nothing about.

GO IT ALONE

Never take anyone with you when shopping if you can possibly help it. You don't save anything by sharing a ride to the grocery store with a friend. She'll only remind you to buy all the specials you don't need and to try the wonderful bread she uses! Go shopping alone even if you have to go in a taxi.

BUYMANSHIP

Buy your meat first. Buy a week's supply at a time because if you don't, you will find that each time you go for meat, you will pick up several other things that you could have done without.

After buying your meat, buy your dairy products. Always be extravagant on eggs, oleo and cheese. These are used for all meals and are wonderful food stretchers.

Try using oleo for frying. Sometimes it is cheaper than shortening.

Never run out of potatoes. They can be cooked many ways and taste good with anything.

If it is agreed that thirty dollars a week should be your allowance for groceries . . . be sure it's really spent for food. Cigarettes, school supplies, aspirin, beer and cough syrup are not food.

To test this, go into the store and buy nothing except food and check out! Then go back in the store and buy those other things. You will find that the real demon in that basket is not what you eat!

If you have a freezer, buy pies, meats, vegetables and anything that is on sale . . . this is a way to save on your budget. When day-old-bread is on sale, buy this, too, and freeze it. It's much cheaper. In one year's time you probably will have saved enough money on groceries to pay for your freezer.

KEEP THE WEEVIL AT BAY

People have written advising the use of bay leaves to discourage weevils. If you put a bay leaf in your flour, corn meal and all such staples, 'tis said you will never have a weevil. I *now* believe this! I tried it and it worked for me. It will cost you a little more than a dime to try it! Bay leaves are cheap.

Or try keeping flour in a plastic bag in the freezer. The bugs keep out and the flour never freezes.

One woman wrote that corn meal was the worst thing to draw weevils. Even if you buy the meal from a trusted store, check it before you use it.

The most inexpensive way to "control" weevils is to put your staples in fruit jars! You can go buy expensive vacuum containers, but if you stop to think about it, there are no better airtight containers than fruit jars. These have been used to pack foodstuffs in for years. They must be good.

Also, with a fruit jar, you can see how much meal and pancake mix you have left when you make your grocery list. This eliminates the "shall I buy another package of oatmeal" puzzle when you make your grocery list.

Fruit jars now have wide tops and these are most convenient for some things. They are easily labeled too. Tear the label off the package and insert it inside the jar. That is what I do. If you are ever in doubt as to what is inside, just fish the label out with a fork.

HOW TO BE AN EGGSPERT

For those who love poached eggs and cannot cook them to perfection, here is the answer to a "perfect egg" that I find leaves no residue in the pan!

Use a skillet to poach three eggs—a pot or pan could be used if only one or two eggs are being cooked—and fill it with one to one and a half inches of water. Do *not* salt. It makes no difference whether the skillet is stainless steel or aluminum. When the water comes to a boil, turn the fire off. Then pour in a "blub-blub" of white or yellow vinegar. Drop your eggs in and do *not* cover.

When these eggs are salted, topped with fresh ground pepper and placed on top of a piece of toast . . . you will have reached perfection. And don't worry—you can't taste the vinegar.

BUDGET THE BACON

Still on that diet? Hubby needs to cut down on his fat intake? Start with bacon—and save, too!

I bought three different kinds of bacon one day. What a difference in bacon . . . even the way it cooks. Now, one pound of bacon had many more slices per package. It was cut thinner. Another pound had the same number of slices but they were shorter and sliced thicker. The third pound had long, narrow slices but they were leaner.

Thin bacon goes farther. And I found that when it was fried, most of the thin bacon didn't have that raw, fatty part left. The thick sliced bacon had more uncooked fat.

Doesn't it stand to reason that the old man is going to eat his two slices of bacon, regardless of size? So why not save on your budget and his calories by buying thin bacon?

Also, I found that paper napkins drain better and absorb more of the excess fat than some other paper products. When you fry bacon, try draining it on two paper napkins. By laying another paper napkin on top of the bacon and pressing it gently while it is still hot, there is more grease absorption. If you wait until the bacon is cold to press between napkins, this may cause it to crumble.

Remember, when you buy thinner bacon, you get more slices in each pound. No need to call this fact to your husband's attention! He might soon ask for three slices!

GIVING HOTCAKES A RUNAROUND

Have you ever tried oval-shaped hotcakes? When you cook them in a round skillet or round grill an oval shape will fit better and you can get more in! And besides . . . who ever said that pancakes had to be round? Grandmother? Oblong hotcakes also fit better on the plate. This leaves space for the bacon without all the syrup spreading into it.

Another hint: if hotcakes stick to the grill, try adding more shortening to the batter.

And did you know that any recipe which says, "and add one egg," could be made better by separating the white and yolk? This includes cakes, waffles, hotcakes, etc. This white, when beaten separately, adds bubbles, tenderness and makes the finished product lighter. This is true for nearly all boxed items.

The next time you have hotcakes, try adding two eggs with the whites and yolks separated. Beat yolks into batter as usual and then whip whites until stiff. *Fold* these egg whites into the batter just before cooking. Even though the recipe calls for one egg . . . try using two.

BE AN "INSTANT" SUCCESS

A well-known, plush restaurant which is famous for its coffee (but won't let me use its name!) uses instant coffee! It's unbelievable to me but the boss swears it's so.

The owner says it's not the instant coffee itself that tastes so different but the way people make it. Here's his secret:

Bring water to a boil, then put instant coffee in the water. Let the water come to a boil again . . . until bubbles come to the top. Immediately turn off the fire. Let coffee sit a minute or two and then pour into cups.

The second boiling is the secret, the owner says. He also says that customers never ask if the restaurant's coffee is instant or not; they just want a second cup.

I just made a cup of coffee for one of my neighbors this way and she says it sure does taste different. I used a stainless steel pan which might have helped, too.

SPEAKING OF COFFEE . . .

A friend of mine suggested using white facial tissues to line the coffee basket when perking coffee. It works wonderfully. It not only filters the coffee but the grounds come out of the basket beautifully.

This is a little hint for those who like half and half in their coffee but find the price rather prohibitive; buy canned or boxed powdered whole milk and follow the directions for mixing. You can mix it up the night before you need it so that it can get real cold.

AND SPEAKING OF CREAMS

When whipping cream with your electric mixer, if you will take a piece of wax paper and tear a little hole in the middle, slip the stem of the beater through the hole and then attach your beater in the machine . . . the cream won't spatter when beating. This piece of wax paper should be large enough to cover the bowl.

For those who feel that nothing can equal old-fashioned whipped cream (I flavor mine with two tablespoons of sugar and half a teaspoon of vanilla), try this: Take a bowl of whipped cream, or any leftover dabs, and drop in mounds on a wax paper lined cookie sheet and freeze until solid! Repack into plastic bags, seal and store in the freezer for future use. Next time you need whipped cream for topping your individual dessert portions . . . place frozen mound on dessert and allow about fifteen minutes for thawing!

Do you know that if you happen to be out of sour cream, a little buttermilk on baked potatoes is every bit as good as sour cream?

IN PRAISE OF PEPPER MILLS

I want to tell you about pepper mills. These are little gadgets for grinding fresh pepper—and, believe me, there's nothing like fresh pepper! You haven't tasted real seasoning until you own a pepper mill. They don't cost too much, either. You can buy little ones, big ones and middle-sized ones. You can buy fresh pepper corns for the mill at any condiment counter. They look like black beads. These you put in your pepper mill and grind. What aroma! Makes all the difference in the world in mashed potatoes and that good gravy! And when you scramble fresh eggs, make spaghetti sauce or cook vegetables . . . use that fresh pepper!

So, splurge with that extra dollar you've got socked away—get a pepper mill. I waited until I was forty to purchase one. Don't you wait that long. Bet you a nickel . . . if you ever taste *fresh* pepper . . . you will love it. It adds so much zip to all your cooking that you can't do without it.

MEMOS FROM THE MISCELLANEOUS FILE

When using oranges for cooking, grate the peel before cutting them. Store in your freezer. Canned or frozen juice may be used with this in any recipe calling for both juice and rind.

Don't ever waste that extra ear of corn. Wrap it in foil and it will keep a few days. Next time you need a fill-in for supper, slice the corn off the ear, boil it in water, and butter. If you need to stretch it, make a fritter batter and fry it. It's also grand in hotcakes for breakfast.

To prevent gummy noodles, rice, macaroni and spaghetti, add two teaspoons of cooking oil to the water before cooking and your problems will be solved. This makes the noodles glisten and stand apart.

Keep a large kitchen salt shaker near the flour canister; it makes a good flour duster for cake pans, meat and fish, etc. It is less messy and doesn't waste flour.

Nearly everyone makes good gravy, but on the days you have no condiments to use . . . you are usually stumped. An answer to this problem is to put some flour in a custard cup or a foil pie pan when roasting meat in the oven. The flour browns slowly as the roast cooks. If it is put in the oven at the same time as the roast it will brown evenly and be ready to make a rich brown gravy when the meat is done.

For working wives who want to defrost meat for dinner, take it out of the freezer in the morning and wrap it snugly in four or five sheets of newspaper. When you return home in the afternoon or evening the meat will be thawed and *still* chilled instead of mushy and warm! Also, the juice will still be in the meat instead of all over the drainboard.

Salad dressing may be used on sandwiches when preparing them ahead of time for the freezer. Also butter or oleo. But frozen mayonnaise has a tendency to separate.

Meat tenderizers (though you may not have noticed it) come in *two* forms! Seasoned and *un*-seasoned. Most companies package both kinds. I personally buy *un*-seasoned. I feel that salt and condiments which come in the more expensive seasoned tenderizers are much cheaper when bought in big boxes. Seasoned tenderizer is not cheap. Look on the next bottle you buy . . . and look for the fine print . . . pick up a bottle that says unseasoned. And did you know that this can be applied to chicken too? It's terrif!

For those who are tired of canned and frozen biscuits . . . bake your own. I make a large batch at a time and bake until slightly underdone. I do *not* let the tops get brown. I then separate them and put the desired number for each meal in foil and freeze. When ready for use, I bake as usual but in the same foil, folding back the top of the foil so the biscuit tops will get brown.

If you put a "squirt of lemon" or a teaspoon of vinegar in the water in which you boil cauliflower, you will find no discoloration. Also . . . are you cooking cauliflower in aluminum? If so, try cooking it in another type pan. Stainless steel, glass, or something else.

Place a heel of bread on top of cabbage before putting the lid on the pot and cooking it . . . there will be *no* odor. The bread has no effect on the cabbage and should be removed after cooking. Good for broccoli and Brussels sprouts too.

THIS ICES UP ANYTHING

How many of you like finely-crushed ice for desserts, drinks, homemade ice cream, cooler boxes and hundreds of other uses, but do not have an ice crusher? Well, rejoice, you lovers of the frozen daiquiri! If you have freezer space tall enough to store a two-quart *plastic* milk carton . . . you're in business!

After you have consumed the milk or fruit juice, rinse out the plastic carton, fill with water and store in the freezer. When ready for that finely crushed ice, remove one or more cartons from the freezer. Next—and this is the trick—take the cartons to a *solid* concrete sidewalk or patio. Holding onto the carton, slam it against the cement on all four sides until it quits going "crack" and starts going "thunk."

Then open the top and pour out the finest crushed ice you have ever seen. It's amazing! This saves getting out the ice bucket too. Another thing good about this method is that you can pour out just as much ice as you need for your iced tea and drinks and then return the carton to the freezing compartment with the unused ice. It also saves filling those messy ice trays and spilling water. The milk carton will not stick to the bottom of the freezing compartment either.

CHEAPER THAN A CHURN

I thought I had heard everything until I got a letter that told how to make buttermilk . . . with few calories. And so cheap, too! You will not believe it until you try it. I didn't at first, but for weeks afterward I practically lived on home-made buttermilk which I now make every night with pow-dered skim milk.

Buy *one* quart of buttermilk and some powdered skim milk. With this one quart of "store-bought" buttermilk, you can make many quarts yourself.

Make up the powdered milk according to the directions on the box. Wash and sterilize pint-size fruit jars. Pour one half cup of buttermilk into each pint jar and fill to the top with the powdered, mixed, skim milk. Add a pinch of salt and cover the jar. Let jar set out on drainboard overnight. In the morn-ing you will have a big jar of buttermilk. All you have to do is stir and chill.

One jar will yield two glasses of buttermilk with some left over—to fill with skim milk and let clabber again the next night. If you can't make more buttermilk right away, the por-tion that is left in the jar should, of course, be kept refriger-ated until ready to make up another batch.

We all like sour milk biscuits and hotcakes but never seem to have the buttermilk to make them with. But you always have a supply on hand when you make your own. I find but-termilk is delicious with a cold luncheon or any time of the day for a pick-me-up and there are few calories to worry about. But most of all, look at the money I am saving!

SHORT CUTS AND COOKING CAPERS

Here's a cooking trick with that favorite all-hours food: hamburgers. Instead of greasing the skillet, sprinkle the bottom of it lightly with salt and then the hamburgers will fry in their own juices. Much tastier!

Add one grated *raw* potato with each pound of ground meat for luscious, juicy hamburgers.

Before opening a can of soup . . . shake well. This mixes the ingredients within the soup. When you add the water, there won't be any lumps, especially in creamed soups.

A little salt sprinkled in the frying pan will keep fat or lard from spattering. This also makes cleaning the range easier.

To keep lettuce and celery fresh longer, keep in paper bags instead of cellophane. Do not remove outside leaves of lettuce or celery until ready to use.

When cooking beans or rice, add a few drops of vinegar or lemon juice to the contents and your aluminum pot will not turn dark. This will not change the taste of your food.

For a new bacon treat: dip bacon slices in beaten egg, then in crushed cracker crumbs, and broil!

Buy large cans of pepper—they are economical. Then pour the pepper into an empty one-pound salt box by using a small funnel. Just remove the plastic shaker part to do this and replace it. When this is later used for filling the pepper shakers, use the spout!

To make gravy without lumps, put about two tablespoons

of flour in a jar that has a tight cover. Add one or more cups of cold water. Shake vigorously before adding the mixture to the juices in your pan. You can use this method even when the recipe calls for putting the flour directly into the brownings before adding water.

When baking anything that has raisins in it and you don't want them to sink to the bottom . . . put the raisins in the top of your flour sifter before adding the flour to the mixture; then put the flour-coated raisins in your batter and they will not sink to the bottom during cooking.

Check paprika for bugs before using. 'Twould be a sad experience if you ruined a beautiful potato salad. By the way . . . I love pimentos but I only use part of a can at one time. If you put the remaining part in a small jar and cover with vinegar and refrigerate them, they will last for a long time.

If you peel more potatoes than you care to cook, cover them with some water to which a few drops of vinegar have been added. Place them in the refrigerator and they will keep three or four days.

I would like to suggest to wives who are low on their budgets to buy dried black-eyed peas. They're good, cheap, and they cook so quickly, too! Put them in water and add one chopped onion and a few slices of bacon. After they have cooked for a while add a little bit of celery salt and table salt and fresh ground pepper to taste. What a change from dried beans!

Use a regular size ice cream scoop when a recipe calls for one-quarter cup of shortening.

Pour the juices from cooked meat into a container and place in the freezer or the freezing unit of your refrigerator. The grease in the juices will quickly rise to the top of the container. Then you can easily spoon or pour off the grease. In a short time you will have a tastier, greaseless gravy.

Lots of people use garlic but don't like to leave the actual bud in their food. I stick a toothpick through the garlic bud before placing it in the food or sauce. Then it's really easy to find when I want to remove it.

REBAKING BAKED POTATOES

Leftover baked potatoes may be reheated by dipping them in hot water and baking again in a moderate oven.

When you're making potato salad and don't like to eat the onions but like the flavor of them . . . cut one big onion in fourths, place in the potato salad and let sit awhile. Before serving the salad, remove the onion. Some people also boil an onion in the water in which they are boiling the potatoes. The potatoes will absorb some of the flavor this way, too.

DO YOU KNOW YOUR ONIONS?

Many recipes call for "half of an onion grated," and then you wonder what to do with the other half! If you don't want to waste it, cut the onion in half *before* peeling it. Peel the first half for immediate use. Place the second half on a plate (or wax paper) with the cut end down and the outside skin still on. Place this in your refrigerator. The next time you need only part of an onion for a salad or recipe, it will be ready for use.

An iced onion, when grated, is wonderful in salads and many other things. Try sliced onions in pickled beets and let them dissolve into the juice. These "dyed" onion rings are wonderful for topping that plain lettuce salad!

To rid your cutting board of onion, garlic or fish smell . . . cut a lime in two and rub the smelly surface with the cut side of the lime, squeezing it as you rub. Even a vegetable brush or sponge that has been used in the kitchen perks up and loses any odor when dipped in lime juice. It works like a charm, even on your hands and nails, and keeps them quite soft. Rinse with tap water afterwards, and that's all there is to it! Another way to remove the onion odor from your hands: run your fingers and palms over a metal knife blade while holding this under cold running water a minute or so.

How many recipes start with: "Cook two slices of bacon until crisp. Brown diced onions in fat . . . "? Save yourself lots of effort and money by preparing two or three diced onions in bacon fat left from breakfast bacon. The actual bacon is seldom vital to the recipe. Keep the onions in the refrigerator. They are also tasty when added to scrambled eggs for breakfast, or to some other dish or vegetable.

BE A GREENS KEEPER

Parsley—that good old stand-by we often need a bit of but never seem to have on hand when we need it—can be frozen! When you buy a fresh bunch in the market, wash it, trim the stems, dry it in a towel and roll it up in foil; then put it in the freezer.

When you need chopped parsley, just remove it from the freezer and grate it. No chopping board is necessary. Grate only the amount you need and put the rest back in the freezer. When kept in this manner, parsley will stay very green and taste the same as when freshly chopped. And did you know that chives, when handled the same way, are excellent? Remove the long slivers of frozen chives and slice off tiny bits when you need them.

Here's what another woman does with parsley: "I buy a bunch of fresh parsley at the market and wash it well. When it is drained of the moisture, I use a pair of scissors or a sharp knife and cut it up finely. I lay the parsley on a flat cookie sheet and spread it out evenly. Since I have a pilot light in my oven, I just set the parsley in the oven and leave it for a few days on the middle rack. The warmth of the oven dries it slowly and leaves it a beautiful green color. When this is completely

dry, I crumble it up and put it in jars, capping them tightly.
If I need to use the oven in the meantime . . . I just remove
the parsley and replace it later. I stir the leaves two or three
times a day."

Dry celery tops by putting them in a paper bag with holes
in it, folding over the top of the bag and letting them sit until
completely dry. An empty salt bag will do the same thing. The
bag can be kept any place that is dry. Parsley and green onion
tops may be dried the same way. Also save carrots and onion
rings and dry them with the same method. These are especially good when you run out of vegetables as they can be
made into wonderful soups. Try simmering these dried vegetables in canned tomato soup and serve with croutons.

CARROTS, CARROTS, CARROTS . . .

Carrots can be cooked thousands of ways according to all
the letters that pour in. Here are some of them:

They may be boiled with the skins on and then the outside
jacket will slip right off without peeling with a knife or peeler
. . . just like a potato. They may be fried. They may be
mashed, baked, broiled, and boiled. They may be shredded in
salads, served in stick form like celery and baked like candied
sweet potatoes. When frying, some people dip in flour, egg
batter and flour again, then roll in breakfast cereal! Many people write that they cook carrots with potatoes and then mash
them all together. Some whip them together. This makes the
potatoes a slight orange color and produces an entirely new
flavor.

TRY THESE

When broiling meats or bacon on a rack . . . place a piece
or two of dry bread in the broiler pan to soak up the dripped
fat. This not only helps to eliminate smoking of the fat but
reduces the chances of the fat catching fire.

If your family spurns the heels of bread, save them in a pie
pan in the oven until you have a good supply. Then crumb
them in the mixer or roll them with a rolling pin. Toss these
in melted fat or butter and save in a plastic bag in your freezer

for that inevitable casserole topping. You can add a few table-spoons of parmesan!

When boiling potatoes, put a little bacon grease or cooking oil in the water to eliminate the sticky ring at the top of the pan. It will not affect the taste of the potatoes.

Wash and tear lettuce for your salads and place in a bowl lined with paper napkins or towels. Place another napkin on top. Set in refrigerator for at least one hour before serving. The excess moisture will be absorbed by the napkins. Your lettuce will be crisp.

Meat loaf will not stick to its pan if you place a strip of bacon at the bottom of the pan before placing your meat loaf in it.

When opening a can of food, always open the end of the can that has been next to the shelf (the bottom of the can). The heavy food that is at the bottom of the can will come out first because of its weight and the rest of the food will pour out easily. Besides, it's cleaner (no dust on top).

When making meat balls . . . always dip your fingers in water before rolling the balls. This will prevent stickiness.

Try making a small roast beef and a small roast pork to-gether. The meats pick up the taste from each other and the gravy is out of this world.

When you want to pulverize a garlic bud, put the bud be-tween two thicknesses of wax paper (skin included) and just hit it several times with a hammer. Presto! . . . it's smashed and the juice is ready to use. No garlic presser or pliers are necessary.

If boxed tomatoes are bought from the grocer a little bit green and are laid in the kitchen window, they will ripen slow-ly and beautifully. Take only the amount of tomatoes out of the refrigerator that you will need in the next day or two and let them ripen slowly. This really changes the taste.

For a good "pan greaser," make a puff from a paper towel.

Take one paper towel and fold in half. Pick up the four corners and hold in the fingers. Give this a twist, leaving a "puff" in the middle and a handle about an inch long with a big puff on the bottom for greasing skillets, etc. The shortening will not come through on the hands as the twisted handle will prevent it from doing so.

When freezing a casserole dish, line your casserole with foil before filling it, then freeze. When it's frozen solid, slip food and foil from the casserole dish, seal tightly and replace in freezer. The dish can be used while the casserole waits! When ready to bake, slip food from foil, place casserole in the same dish and bake.

When baking potatoes, I find it a wonderful idea to put each potato in one of the holes in a muffin tin. The tin makes it easy to remove the potatoes from the oven and keeps them from rolling around or dropping through the racks in the oven.

Here is an old faithful timesaver: When cooking mashed potatoes I cut a few raw potatoes into "French fry" style with my handy little French fry cutter. This way, all pieces cook uniformly and quickly, with no possible chance of lumping, which I feel is due to some pieces being undercooked because of the difference in sizes.

Beans must be washed, and I have found that all those little so-called "rocks" in beans aren't rocks at all, but little pieces of dirt. So . . . now I put the beans in my flour sifter and turn on the faucet and let the water run. This washes the beans and dissolves those little hard pieces of dirt at the same time. Sure beats "picking beans" the old-fashioned way!

To avoid the yellow ring around the center of a hard boiled egg: as soon as the egg is finished simmering (and never boil an egg rapidly), pour off the hot water and immediately cover it with cold water to stop the cooking of the egg.

In broiling a steak, line the shallow roasting pan with aluminum foil. A nice brown gravy will form and you'll be saved washing and scouring the pan.

When cutting marshmallows or chopping dates, if you dip your scissors in water and cut them wet, the goodies won't stick.

Did you know that you could take any boxed cake and add one-quarter cup of cooking oil and it would be just like the one grandmother used to make? Do not use any more as the cake will be so tender that it will fall apart.

For those who have small families and hate to bake big cakes—bake and ice the cake completely. After the icing sets, cut the cake in pieces and lay on paper plates. Cover and freeze them. This way you will have no stale cake, as the pieces can be thawed individually.

When rolling cookie dough, use powdered sugar instead of flour on your board. This will make your cookies a wee bit sweeter but they will not get tough as they sometimes do when they are rolled out on a floured board.

PRESTO! PIE!

Pies are so good, but they take so much time to bake due to all the separate steps involved.

Here is a short cut: *Never* make one pie crust at a time. Always make at least four. Cook, cool and place one on top of the other in the pans they were baked in. Cover with wax paper or put in a big paper sack and fold end under.

Place on any high shelf. These will stay crisp for weeks. Then, when company arrives unexpectedly or you don't have a big dinner and need a fill-in, cook any boxed pudding or take any can of already prepared pie filling and put this in the pie crust. Your pie is ready! No trouble at all. For topping, use the boxed meringue, whipped cream or ice cream. Making the four crusts at one time will save many hours of labor, and most of all, . . . cleaning up three extra messes.

For those delicious pumpkin pies we all love so well . . . the great disappointment is a soggy undercrust.

To avoid this, prepare the pie crust in the usual manner and line the pie plate. *Then* turn the oven to the highest temperature recommended in your recipe to "set" the crust and put the unfilled shell in the oven for ten minutes while you finish preparing the filling.

When you remove the pie shell from the oven it will not be brown (perhaps a little colored). Pour in the filling and turn the thermostat to the proper cooking temperature for the custard and relax. The pie crust will be crisp, even for the "dividend" the next day.

A dietician sent me the answer to the "weeping meringue" problem. For a nine-inch pie use three egg whites, one-quarter teaspoon cream of tartar, six tablespoons of sugar and, if desired, one-half teaspoon of flavoring. Beat egg whites at *room temperature* with cream of tartar until frothy. *Gradually* beat in the sugar, a little bit at a time. Continue beating until stiff and glossy.

Pile meringue onto pie filling, being careful to seal the meringue onto all the edges of the crust to prevent shrinking. If any of the filling is exposed to the heat (is not entirely covered) it may cause "weeping." When meringue is brown, cool it in a slightly warm place away from drafts. A sudden chill may make the meringue fall. And it's best to remember that baking too long (eight to ten minutes at 400 degrees is long enough) and incomplete blending of the sugar are the causes of "weeping."

Also . . . I received two letters from famous restaurants that said the secret of their high meringue was adding baking powder to the room temperature egg whites before beating! I tried this and it's so. It seems to "swell" the meringue and make it higher. I often wondered how a restaurant could afford so many eggs! No special amount of baking powder was given . . . just a "bit"! I used a half-teaspoon. One hotel chef wrote that the secret was never to "dump" in the sugar. He said he was the baker and made all the pies. He makes big batches of meringue at a time. He said he sprinkles the sugar in small amounts while operating his electric beater.

One baker wrote and said he used one-half cup of sugar to three egg whites. This makes a thicker meringue. He also wrote that meringue should be baked on the highest shelf in an oven. This way the meringue browns without heating the custard and browning the pie crust too much. I used one-half cup of sugar and found it much better on the second meringue. I found that it was thicker, higher, tastier, and had more body.

PUTTING CRUST ON CHICKEN

A woman asked me if there is any way to get a crust on fried chicken after removing the skin. Her husband insists that she remove the skin from chicken breasts.

I advised her: Remove the skin from the chicken if your husband does not like it. Soak the chicken in water. I add salt if I am using frozen chicken, but you may not want to. When the chicken is thoroughly thawed and warm, remove it from the water, and quickly put it in a bed of flour. *Nothing else!* Leave it there a few seconds.

Remove the chicken (after it's floured on all sides) and lay it on a piece of wax paper. Leave it there for at least thirty minutes. This will form a seal and will look as if you had put glue on the chicken. It will not look too appetizing. Never mind. This is exactly what you want. It is *most important* to let the chicken sit thirty minutes after flouring.

This odd-looking batter (and it won't look like batter at all, but a real mess) will form a coating on the chicken that I find seals the juices *in* and keeps the grease *out* when frying! Really it does.

One day, all my neighbors came in and we fried over fifty chicken breasts in different kinds of oils, grease and shortenings. We used deep friers, stainless steel, aluminum and an old cast iron skillet. The comparisons were amazing. All agreed that nothing could beat the old cast iron skillet. Seems as if the heat spreads slowly through the cast iron.

Place your chicken in hot shortening about one inch deep and *immediately* put the lid *on!* Have the fire on medium heat. Never cook chicken too fast. It gets brown on the outside before the inside has a chance to cook. When the chicken is golden brown on one side, turn each piece over *once.* We found that turning chicken pieces over more than once made it greasy.

When the chicken is done (especially if you are frying a lot of it) place it in a pressure cooker (with the grate in) to keep it warm until you are finished frying it all. As you remove it from your frying pan, and place it in a big Dutch oven, or the pressure cooker, *then and only then* salt it.

You will find that you have the most beautiful crust on your chicken that you have ever seen on home-fried chicken! You will not know that the skin has been removed. (Most people remove the skin to get rid of the fat particles. That's the reason I do.)

And, ladies, I am going to let you in on a secret that we discovered in that neighborhood chicken-fry. Now that it's tried and tested . . . I will pass it on.

We found that when using shortening to fry chicken, if you put a few drops of yellow cake coloring in the shortening *after* the shortening heats, it will give your chicken the most beautiful color you have ever seen! Truly! It's a golden yellow and looks as if it had been fried in pure butter! Cake coloring is cheap. Buy some and try it. Get the small bottles with different colors. They cost about twenty-five cents for four colors, and can be used for many things.

As I said, my neighbors and I tried all the batter recipes, egg dips, buttermilk, etc. . . . and none was so good as a plain water soak, quickly dipped in pure flour and set aside for thirty minutes. Don't shake the water off the chicken before dipping it in the flour. You need this to form the "seal" to keep the juices in the chicken and the grease out.

And don't ask me what we did with all that fried chicken. All the neighbors had chicken for dinner, lunches next day, and right now we are sick of chicken. But we sure found out there were differences in methods of chicken-frying!

WHY NOT COOK DINNERS BY THE DOZENS?

Make your own freezer dinners the easy way! Make 'em by the dozens . . . it's cheaper.

Make portions large for Daddy, regular for you and *small* for Mary and Johnnie. No need to waste food. Label each one.

Fill that freezer yourself when you're in the mood to really cook. Then on the days you wash and iron, just pop the meals into the oven.

This is the way to do it: I never cook one roast any more. I always cook two or three and sometimes even four. *After* they cool, slice and set aside the meat while you make your gravy. Let the gravy partially cool, too, as you should never put any hot food into your freezer.

The TV trays should be scalded if you have no dishwasher. Turn them on edge in your drainer and let the hot water run over them. For those who have dishwashers, just put the trays in and run through the rinse cycle and leave them in the washer until ready for use. These trays do not have to be dried. Moisture is good when you pack them.

Now, you have cooked all these beef roasts and they are sliced. You will have some pretty slices that look just like the picture books and some small pieces. So why not look professional as long as you are packing them? Put the small pieces on the bottom and lay the prettiest piece on top. Put the chunks in another pot for later. Pour a big spoon of gravy (and this should be rather thin for freezing) on top of this lovely sliced beef.

DON'T FORGET THE COLOR!

You have two compartments in the tray yet to fill. I have said many times that you can learn to cook by color. You need something red and green at each meal. Fill your trays with color. The easiest way I have learned to fill freezer-dinner trays is with canned vegetables. They are cheap and one medium can will fill four to five trays. Use 'em. After all, you cooked the beef . . . don't tire yourself out by trying to cook all your vegetables, too.

Put green peas or string beans in one compartment. In the other try to use something orange. Try carrots or sweet potatoes. You can use mashed white potatoes (if you make 'em thin) and use only one colored vegetable. If you use white potatoes, put a pat of yellow margarine on top. It will melt and give color when the dinner is baked. I put one tablespoon of vegetable juice in each vegetable. If there is no juice, I put in water. This is what makes it "steam" and keeps it moist when it bakes.

THE ASSEMBLY LINE

Now line up about six trays on the drainboard and get to work. (Fill only six at a time.) Place pats of butter or oleo on top of the vegetables before covering them with heavy foil. When these six are finished . . . place six more on down the drainboard and fill them.

Cut foil squares longer than the trays so the foil will fold over the edges. I have found that if I use my ink marker and mark the top of the foil *before* covering the tray, it is easier. I label these with the names of all the vegetables and meats, as: "Beef, pot. (for potatoes), peas." I put "child" on the label for smaller portions. Then I know how many frozen dinners to take out of the freezer and which ones!

"MAIN DISH" LEFTOVERS

The chunks of beef that are left over, I barbecue. This takes very little time and can be done while you are filling the beef trays. The beef can either be chopped up or left in hunks or small slices. With the barbecue trays, I always use Mexican chili beans and strawberry-applesauce or fried rice or pickled beets. When serving these barbecue dinners, all you need is a salad for something green. Color again! Don't try to make your own Mexican beans. Beans in the can are cheap and can be put directly into that tray after opening. So can the applesauce and beets.

COUNT YOUR PENNIES

Each tray can be varied by using different canned vegetables. I stick mainly to the things that are inexpensive and bake well:

Butter beans (for 15 cents, why cook beans for two hours!), shoe peg corn, canned sweet potatoes, beets, canned figs (these are terrific when they are hot), canned spaghetti, canned macaroni and cheese sauce, string beans, peas, etc.

If you like to make your own macaroni dinner . . . it's quick, cheap and easy, too. The water can boil while you are sterilizing your trays. Macaroni only takes a few minutes and it's done. Too, this can be mixed with any leftover barbecued beef and it's good.

If you must make your own macaroni and cheese . . . try the sea shell macaroni for variety. What's left over can be made into a salad for dinner.

Turkeys are wonderful, too, in frozen dinners. They are comparatively inexpensive and go a long way. The day you buy a turkey . . . buy a big one! Why cook something all afternoon if it will only be eaten in thirty minutes?

The bigger a turkey is, the cheaper it is. Those bones weigh, too! Don't forget that! As long as you are going to buy bones you might as well get a bird with lots of meat! It takes very little more cooking time and *no* more energy.

Make the leftovers into frozen turkey dinners. This day you will make dressing . . . that's all . . . because you will open those cans to fill the compartments in the tray.

For instance, I cooked one big turkey and made dressing, opened canned sweet potatoes and sprinkled them with brown sugar and added a pat of oleo; opened a can of peas and put a spoon of juice and a pat of oleo on top of them, poured gravy over the turkey and dressing, and had twenty-four turkey dinners ready for the freezer. Easy! Think of the nights I won't have to cook dinner!

Besides, it's mighty nice the days you do your laundry and ironing not to have to worry about "what's for supper" and dinner dishes and all those pots and pans. If you're tired, try popping a frozen dinner into the oven on these days for lunch. What a feeling it is to *know* these good dinners are in your freezer "just in case" you have company, get sick, or just want to be lazy one day . . . without a guilty feeling!

BUT, PLEASE NOTE . . .

Here are a few hints to be remembered:

Meat should never be cut while hot when packing freezer dinners. It slices better when cold, without tearing, and looks prettier.

For those who like meat cooked in the fat (I do), but cannot eat fat or don't like it . . . fat should be removed while the roast is barely warm! You can take a knife and scrape the warm fat off the meat without losing any of the meat itself.

If you don't have freezer trays ask one of your friends to save hers for you. Lots of people buy frozen dinners and throw the trays away. They'll be happy to save 'em for you.

Heloise's Barbecue Sauce

¼ cup grated onion	¼ cup fresh lemon juice
1 tablespoon fat	2 tablespoons brown sugar
½ cup water	1 cup chili sauce
2 tablespoons vinegar	1 teaspoon chili powder
1 tablespoon Worcestershire sauce	salt and pepper to taste

Place all ingredients in a large saucepan and cook over medium heat twenty minutes. *Note:* Do *not* substitute catsup for chili sauce, or *anything* for the fresh lemon juice in this recipe. The result will not be satisfactory.

This sauce can be used for basting barbecued spareribs, chicken, or can be added to leftover roast beef for frozen dinners. If you have too much sauce for one batch of roast, put the extra sauce in a tightly covered jar and store in your refrigerator or freezer.

FOR SPAGHETTI LOVERS

A woman wrote me that she could never please her husband as she either cooked his spaghetti too hard or too soft. Finally, she found the answer: "And so now I pick up a piece of spaghetti on a fork. I stand back a little bit and throw it at the wall. If it sticks . . . it's perfect. If it falls off . . . it ain't done! Needs more cooking!" (I don't advocate throwing spaghetti against the wall for testing, but we did try it and the woman is right!)

A "spaghetti expert" sent in the following: "I am from Italy. I was raised on spaghetti. There are over a hundred ways to cook it and mix it with different sauces.

"Most cooks seem to have problems. Being in the restaurant business and 'on call' to serve spaghetti at any hour, I feel qualified to give the following advice:

"I cook batches of spaghetti at a time and serve it with meat sauce, meat balls, etc. Recipes vary on sauces but the answer is—if the spaghetti is correctly cooked . . . the sauce is always accepted.

"*Never* overcook spaghetti. Cook it in lots of boiling water to which salt and some cooking oil have been added. This will 'glaze' the spaghetti and keep it from sticking together. It should also keep the pot from boiling over.

"As soon as the spaghetti is done [test by pinching a piece of it under cold running water . . . not by throwing it on a wall], blanch immediately in cold water! This is the secret, and it stops the cooking immediately.

"If spaghetti is left in any part of the warm water and not cooled quickly, it will continue cooking to some extent. This ruins real spaghetti.

"If one of your housewives is having a party or her family is late for dinner, tell her to leave the spaghetti in the cold water; it doesn't make any difference if it is left one or six hours. Place it in a glass or stainless steel bowl and be sure it is completely covered with cold water. This will keep in the refrigerator for two days.

"When ready for use (after storing it) bring a pot of water to a rolling boil (but first add a little more cooking oil and some salt) and with the spaghetti in a sieve or colander, dip it under the water for a few minutes, drain and it's ready for your sauce!

"Always salt the water in which the spaghetti is reheated and add a bit of oil. This brings freshness to it.

"This is a good method to use when you housewives are having a party and want to make the spaghetti and sauce a day or two ahead of time. This way you won't be tired when company arrives. Restaurant owners always do this. Why shouldn't you wives?"

Here's a spaghetti sauce which a cook sent us from one of the most famous hotels in the United States:

¼ cup of olive oil	3 tablespoons fresh parsley
1 cup finely chopped onions	chopped fine
4 cloves of garlic chopped fine	fresh ground black pepper

1 cup canned tomatoes	1 teaspoon salt
(or 1 cup of canned	½ teaspoon dry crushed red
tomato juice)	pepper
2 tablespoons of tomato paste	2 ounces red wine
1 finely chopped carrot	1 cup of tomato purée
½ cup butter	2 stalks of finely chopped
1 pound of ground beef	celery
4 strips finely chopped bacon	

Warm olive oil in a sauce pan over low heat. Add butter and simmer until melted. Add onion and sauté until golden brown. Add ground beef and bacon; sauté until brown, stirring occasionally.

Add garlic, parsley, salt, black pepper and red pepper. Cook over low heat for at least ten minutes. Add wine, cover and steam for a few minutes more.

Then . . . add tomatoes, purée and paste. Bring to boiling point, add celery and carrots. Cover and cook over very low heat for one hour, stirring occasionally. Serves four.

This can be varied to suit your own taste. I have tried it many ways. We especially like it with one teaspoon of each of the following added: Worcestershire sauce, vinegar and chili powder.

I have made this sauce without the meat and dropped meat balls into the sauce after frying them. Real yummy!

SUDDEN THOUGHT

And, ladies, did you know that when something says . . . "chop very fine" . . . you can *grate* it much easier? Get your graters out and grate onions, fresh parsley, garlic (canned tomatoes, too . . . they go through the grater like magic!) and use the carrot last. This will clean your grater.

RECIPE FROM CHINA

Here's just what you have been waiting for—a new way to cook beef. Wait till you smell it cooking . . . then taste it . . . then eat it!

Know what it is? It's Peking Roast!

This recipe is for cheap cuts of roast beef and when cooked in coffee . . . it's terrific! Use boiling beef, chuck, brisket, etc.

I learned how to cook cheap cuts of beef this way when we

lived for a while in Peking, China. One hotel is famous for its tender beef and I finally learned the secret . . . so I am passing it on.

I have found that if I mix two different cuts of beef and cook them at the same time, the result is even better. I, personally, like a boiling beef and a brisket. Those who like all lean meat can eat the brisket but yet get the flavor from the boiling beef.

Take any three-to-five-pound roast and use a large knife to cut slits completely through the meat. They will look like little tunnels. Insert slivers of garlic and onion into these slits. Onions alone may be used if you do not like the taste of garlic. If you prefer it without either, that's all right too.

Put the beef in a bowl and pour one cup of vinegar over it, making sure that the vinegar runs down into the little slits. Place this in your refrigerator for from twenty-four to forty-eight hours.

When ready to cook the roast, discard the vinegar solution and place meat in a heavy pot (iron if possible) and brown in oil until *nearly* burned on both sides. Then pour two cups of strong black coffee over the roast. Add two cups of water and cover.

Cook this *slowly* at a simmer for six hours on top of the stove. Do *not* season with anything else until twenty minutes before serving and then add salt and pepper. That's all!

Girls, your roast will fall apart with the touch of a fork, no matter how tough the meat originally was.

In Peking, they add one-half a cup of gin or whiskey to the boiling mixture but this may be omitted.

And wait until you taste that yummy black gravy! It may be thickened or left as is. If you like lots of gravy, some water may be added.

Another thing . . . if you cook your roast too fast or if the lid on your pot is not tight enough . . . you may need some additional water. Never add more than one cup of water at a time.

I've been cooking Peking Roast for years and every time I make it the platter is licked clean! Another good thing about it—when making it for company, it can be made ahead of time and never fails. The beautiful black meat is something different and everyone will ask you for your recipe!

The meat is usually served with big baked potatoes, green peas, and cranberry sauce.

SAVE BOTH TIME AND MONEY

Now I am going to talk about time savers and budget savers for the average housewife.

Hamburger is the cheapest meat most persons can buy. I'm going to tell you an easy way to fix it and save time, too.

I found that buying hamburger when it is on sale at bargain prices and then freezing it, is profitable timewise. You use less energy if the hamburger is made up immediately into different things before being frozen for future use. It can be made up into meat balls, meat loaves, hamburger patties and spaghetti sauce. The time-saving idea was uppermost in my mind. Later on, as I fried the hamburger, cooked the meat loaves, and used the meat balls, I appreciated how really wonderful this idea was. As I came across the same old question, "What's for supper?" . . . and thought about the frozen hamburgers that could be cooked immediately without thawing . . . it was terrific!

Divide fresh hamburger when you buy it (I bought six pounds on special sale) and press some of it into patties. Place pieces of wax paper between each patty. Put these inside a plastic bag and freeze them. All you have to do when you are ready to cook them is hit them on the side of the drain board and they fall apart. Fry these immediately.

Put the remaining hamburger in a mixing bowl. You may grate one big onion into this for each pound of hamburger and mix. Add one egg for each pound; salt, pepper, and any other seasonings that you might care for. I used chili powder and Worcestershire in part of this. I divided it into two parts.

Make some of this mixture into meat loaves (if you like bread crumbs in your meat loaf, add now). You should make one big meat loaf and a few small ones. Use these small ones when you are pressed for time. They cook quickly. Use the big one when you have plenty of time to thaw it.

All I do when I am ready to cook these is thaw, add a little catsup (or chili sauce or canned tomatoes), some water, and place in the oven! Now . . . another time saver: when you are baking meat loaves, always place baking potatoes in the oven at the same time and utilize this heat. Open a can of biscuits, pop in the oven, and dinner is ready!

I have found, too, that little individual meat loaves can be made in muffin tins. These cook in less than half the time that a large one will take. Even if you are not pressed for time, try this method once, for a change.

When freezing these, I place cookie liners in each muffin tin, pat the meat loaf to shape, freeze, and then . . . *remove* the liner and all from the muffin tin and pack in plastic bags. This leaves me with a muffin pan for other things—clean and ready for use. When ready to cook, remove the paper, place loaves in the same pan and cook as usual.

What is left of this meat should be made into meat balls and/or spaghetti sauce. These are always good. Roll into balls, place on cookie sheets and freeze. Remove when frozen and place in a plastic bag.

I also found that the meat balls can be placed in ice trays for good freezing. They can be rolled in crumbs when thawed along with canned, little whole potatoes for a good, quick meal. Drain potatoes on paper towels, roll in flour, salt and pepper, add a sprinkle of paprika, and fry them.

By putting meat balls in plastic bags to freeze, you can remove as many as you need at one time! Thus, you save dirty bowls and a messy kitchen.

And . . . do you know that you can separate, make and freeze all these recipes in less than thirty minutes? But best of all it eliminates that last-minute worrying over "what's for supper?"

TRY THIS ONE FOR TENDERNESS

I have tested so many recipes for tender meat balls that today you can just call me "Miss Meatball!"

One of the recipes that came to my attention surpasses all that I have tested. The meat balls are so tender and different that I recommend that you try them.

Hamburger Fluffs

1 pound of ground beef	2 tablespoons flour
½ teaspoon of Worcestershire	½ teaspoon pepper
1 teaspoon salt	2 slices of bread
½ large onion, minced	pinch marjoram
pinch thyme	1 cup evaporated milk
1 egg, whole	

Mix all ingredients. Cover bowl and let stand in refrigerator for a few hours. Form into small balls and brown in cooking oil.

Do not overcrowd. These may be cooked immediately but the secret of the fluffy texture is in waiting.

USE SPOONS FOR THIS

I have learned another secret in making meat balls: Don't roll 'em with your hands. Use two teaspoons. Pick up some of the meat with one teaspoon, and mash it with the other spoon to form a ball. This will make an oblong meat ball. Never mind the shape . . . it's better that way. The meat ball will be the shape of an oyster and will have a very rough texture which will pick up and hold the meat sauce!

This sounds like a lot of trouble but, believe me, it is twice as quick as rolling the balls once you get the hang of it.

Double this recipe and fry all meat balls one day, freezing half of them. The next time you want spaghetti, just thaw 'em and place in your sauce. So easy, so different and—so tender!

SALAD DRESSING—WITH A DIFFERENCE!

The best recipe for salad dressing that has ever come to my attention is made with chives. I make up huge amounts of it at a time and pour this into empty salad dressing bottles. This

dressing is ever-so-good when poured over tossed lettuce salads. It's sweet and sour.

Hot Pepper Catsup Dressing

½ cup sugar
½ cup oil
1 clove garlic, cut in half
¼ teaspoon celery salt

½ cup vinegar
½ cup hot pepper catsup
1 tablespoon chopped chives
salt and pepper to taste

Mix all the above ingredients, then let sit overnight. Remove garlic buds and pour dressing into bottles. Keep in refrigerator. The longer this sits, the better it is.

TAKE A NEW LOOK AT AN OLD FRIEND

I have experimented with tuna . . . that good old stand-by when budgets are tight.

Tuna comes in at least three basic "styles" . . . solid pack, (which means a filet or whole piece), chunks (which means big hunks of the fine meat), and flakes (which means little pieces).

Now . . . tell me this. Why do we buy the most expensive kind, which is solid pack, and spend our energy breaking it up into little pieces for salads or mashing it with a fork for sandwiches? Chunks, which is the next expensive type, could be used in salads and casseroles if you wanted chunks but the cheapest of all is flakes. Why even buy chunk tuna if you are going to spend time mashing it up for sandwiches? Save that money, energy and time and buy flakes in the first place.

When I went through a tuna plant not too long ago, I learned many things I had never known before. When it says "fresh pack" on a can . . . the tuna is cooked and packed without ever being frozen. Some tuna is frozen solid when caught at sea, before being brought to shore.

Some people do not like the taste of tuna; they say they can taste it for hours after eating it. I have found that there are several kinds of packing; some is packed in oil and others in brine. Perhaps the heavy oil is what you are tasting, although many people enjoy that flavor; or you might prefer the new tuna packed in corn oil. Many of us are on diets and trying to get away from so much oil. If you cannot find tuna packed in "brine" try the following method:

Open the can of tuna, leaving the lid *on* the can. Turn the can sideways and squeeze the oil out, using the lid as a "masher," or pour the tuna fish in a potato ricer. I use the ricer, which can be bought at any dime store. It gets more of the oil out.

Many people put the tuna in a colander or big sieve and run warm water over it, then wash the oil out, gently squeezing the tuna to get the excess fluid out. I have tried all ways many times.

After you have the drained tuna in a bowl, grate one apple into the fish on your small grater, then add mayonnaise. The apple makes the tuna taste so different that you will be surprised. Many people have told me that this is the only way they can possibly eat tuna! Funny, the apple doesn't taste, either.

Another way to prepare tuna salad is to add the juice of two fresh lemons to the tuna and mix well before adding mayonnaise. Sweet, chipped pickle relish also enhances the taste, too. And it's odd, but you can't taste the lemon juice, either!

When tuna is drained in any of the above fashions, it can also be made into wonderful tuna croquets. Tuna, when served in salads, is always better served chilled.

So, have tuna tonight. As the English say, "You Americans eat too much. You should have salads more often and rest your stomachs!" And you know, maybe we should!

REFRIGERATOR REMINDER

Several layers of newspapers placed on each shelf when defrosting your refrigerator will help sop up the water and eliminate a lot of sponging.

To prevent mildew on refrigerator gaskets and also inside, wipe with pure vinegar. The acid kills the mildew fungus.

A little vanilla poured on a piece of cotton and placed in the refrigerator will eliminate odors.

When preparing a refrigerator for storage, wash it thoroughly with a strong solution of baking soda and water. Wipe it as dry as possible with a terry cloth towel. Apply ordinary talcum powder to all rubber parts and rub in well, especially in cracks. Either sprinkle fresh coffee grounds loosely on the inside bottom of the refrigerator or place an open container inside with about a half cup of grounds in it. This will keep the refrigerator smelling fresh.

For "leaking" refrigerator doors, where the rubber gasket has rotted: Test this yourself, before calling a repairman, by taking a dollar bill (of course, if you have a ten spot, use it, but it won't tell you any more than a buck will!) and placing it in the door. Close the door gently (this means be sure your hand is out of it) and see if the dollar bill will pull out. Sometimes you can slide it up and down. Do this all along the door from top to bottom. If the bill pulls out or slips when the door is closed . . . then the gasket is bad and should be replaced. Gaskets can be purchased through your local dealer.

2.

Make a Clean Sweep of It!

~~~~~~

THE ORGANIZATION WOMAN

I just finished cleaning my linen closet. I have been cleaning such closets for years and only recently learned how!

Everything in the closet should be removed. Not one shelf at a time, but all at once. And don't plan on doing anything else for the day. If you get that done, you'll be exhausted!

Stack all the sheets in one pile, bath towels in another, and so on down the line. Now, go through each pile and unfold everything. Look it over carefully. Ask yourself, "How long has it been since I used this? I wonder if this sheet is worth

patching? Is it beyond that stage?" (If it is, you can make wonderful pillows slips from these sheets, from the unworn parts, and these can be made in less than three minutes.) Tell yourself, "They haven't used orchid dresser scarves since I was a child. This towel is so worn, I am ashamed to hang it up!"

Make these decisions quickly. That is the secret to easy housekeeping. Never think back. Stop cleaning your house the way it was done generations ago. This is a new age. Don't work yourself into "six feet underground."

You should have three piles of linens. One to be repaired (place that in one pile for later mending—*don't* put it back), one to be discarded, and one to be returned to the closet.

Before arranging your linen, think! What do you use the most? Sheets? No! And where were your sheets? On the most convenient shelf, I'll bet. Where were your towels? Too high for the kiddies to reach? Where were the wash cloths? Separated from the towels? Where were the tablecloths? The pillow slips?

Before you start, think again! Then put back only the things that you use which need no repairs.

Place bath towels in first. Put these in the most convenient place, about waist level. Why? Because the children can get them easily and they are the most used items in your linen closet. If you don't have children, it is a fact that a man can never find anything, and he will see them here. On the same shelf put wash cloths (for the same reasons) and hand towels. These are the most used items and should have top priority when it comes to space. On the shelf above the towels, place the sheets and pillow cases. These are used only once a week. You can afford to reach a bit higher for them. On the top shelf, put odds and ends such as tablecloths, fancy guest towels and place mats.

Now—use any old pencil or crayon and mark on the edge of each shelf what each stack contains, such as double sheets, twin, wash cloths, and so forth. The marks can be erased later if you change your mind.

Go clean that linen closet now, while you are in the mood. Oh, what a wonderful feeling to be able to drag out a sheet without a hole in it and find a bath towel in its proper place!

MAD AT THE WORLD? CLEAN YOUR CLOSETS!

How disorderly and messy are your other closets, and those drawers? Awful, like mine?

Well, I have learned something. *Never* clean a closet or drawer when you are not angry or in the throwing-away mood! You will be wasting your time. I know. I have cleaned for years and always end up with the same things that were in there in the first place . . . minus the dust!

Wait until you are angry! This is the best time to clean. You will say to yourself, "I have kept this dress for two years thinking that I would remake it, but I am so angry today, why not throw it out?" That is your best day to clean. Get rid of "garbage." If you get rid of the excess things, your closets and drawers will be easier to keep. This is what all house-wives are looking for. The easy way!!! It will never be easy if you keep all these things you think you may remake some-day.

Discard the stuff. Give it away. Sell it! Gather it all to-gether (and include that old lawn mower in your garage or the extra household articles) and get rid of them by placing an ad in the paper. You will make a few dollars on the side. One of your neighbors can get together with you and you can dispose of all this excess one way or another. I bet your storage closet looks like mine did! Go through the closets and the garage.

Line clothes closet shelves and replace only the articles which you have worn in the last year. Evening dresses and clothes which are too good to discard, take from that "daily closet" and put in your storage closet. Then fill it with moth balls. These once-a-year-clothes only crowd your other clothes and wrinkle them. They also keep the air from circulating.

When cleaning a clothes closet, remove everything and lay it on the bed. Then clean your closet with a vacuum or broom. Wipe the walls with a disinfectant.

Now . . . start to replace the garments. One by one, look them over and decide, "Should I keep this?" Remember, if you haven't used it in a year . . . you probably never will.

GET RID OF DUST-CATCHERS

How many books do you have that you won't ever use again? Here is just something else to dust and clutter up your room. Go through the books and pick out the ones that you will use again (or think you will).

What to do with the others? Give them to your school or to your neighborhood library. They welcome books. Why not let others have the pleasure of reading them when you are finished with them?

Bric-a-brac? Something else to clutter the house. Why dust around six items on each table when you could dust around two? What is on your coffee table? And end tables?

Gather all the stuff you can't afford to part with and put it in a closet. If it is valuable or sentimental, keep it. Then, once in a while, for variety, change the things you keep out.

Simplicity is the style today. All that is needed on an end table is a lamp, an ash tray and one good piece of bric-a-brac. Keep it simple. It's easier.

DON'T BLAME LACK OF HELP

What about that cedar chest? Have you gone through it lately? Clean it out and discard the things you haven't used in years. You probably never will use them.

You might say, "But I don't have servants. If I did, my house wouldn't be so disorderly." This is not so. A servant cannot throw things away and clean your closets. No one but the head of a household can do this. And that is you.

System is what is needed in housekeeping. If we can't find a system, then the thing to do is get rid of excess things. The less we have, the easier it is to clean.

LEARN TO "TOP-CLEAN"

Here's a review on housecleaning: Remove breakfast dishes and put them to soak in hot water and detergent, make the beds, pick up papers and empty ash trays into a big paper sack you carry around. Heat coffee. While it is heating, douse toilet tissue with rubbing alcohol and wipe the bathroom fixtures. Use a carpet sweeper to "hit" the middle of the floors, take a feather duster to the coffee tables, then go back and do the dishes.

Coffee hot? Drain the pot! You'll get real satisfaction in knowing that your house is at least "top-cleaned."

It is not really the dirt that makes you nervous. It is the mess and disorganization of a home.

Learn to get the "effect and appearance" of being neat as quickly as you can and then the actual dirt and dust will not bother you so much. It's easier to clean things then, too.

I am taking all the letters that have come in and using the best advice from them to get the job done "quickly."

The first thing to do in the mornings is to put your dishes in the sink to soak and then make the beds! I don't know why, but this is most important. It gives a woman a feeling of not being embarrassed if a neighbor drops in, and you're in a better mood, since what has yet to be done doesn't show.

After the beds are made, pick up the newspapers and magazines which your family has strewn all over the house. This takes only a few minutes. If you have children, train them to leave their rooms clean and to make their beds.

Never walk down a long hall more often than necessary. Place objects which belong in another room at the door. Next time you go to that room, take the objects with you.

If you live in a two-story house, never go down the stairs just to put something away. Leave it at the top stair and wait until you have to go down. Then take it with you. The same applies for things that go upstairs. Leave them near the bottom step. Next time you go upstairs, pick them up. This doesn't make your house disorderly.

YOU DON'T NEED EXPENSIVE EQUIPMENT

Now . . . let's discuss some cheaper aids that give us the results we want, yet save our energy.

The first two are a feather duster and a carpet sweeper. These can be obtained with trading stamps or purchased cheaply. For girls who hate housework or who don't have the time for it, these are most important.

Another thing that is important is a chamois (the kind your husband uses to wash the car) to wipe mirrors and glass doors with. If you can't afford an expensive one, buy a cheap one. Other equally important aids are an old wash rag (wonderful for dusting), oil rags and a paper sack. When you use your dust cloth, sprinkle a *little* water on it. This allows you to dust twice as fast. And it picks up spots.

TAKE A SACK WITH YOU

One thing: never walk into a room you are going to clean without a paper sack . . . a big one.

Empty ash trays and throw papers into the sack. You will be amazed at the energy you save by carrying a sack from room to room with you. Magazines . . . letters . . . broken toys that Dennis has left on the floor . . . that stocking with the run . . . hubby's sock with the hole which you will never mend.

Go around the room and clean each coffee and end table. Carry the feather duster with you and dust as you go. Wipe all tables with the oil rag and carry that sack *with* you so you can empty ash trays at the *same* time that you are discarding things.

Use the carpet sweeper on days that you want to clean the house quickly. It is great! Until you get one, you will never know.

Put the paper sack, mop, dust cloth and feather duster at the door leading to the next room you plan to clean as soon as you are through using each item. This saves many steps. Each room may be done this way. Psychologically, you will *think* you are a better housekeeper . . . and feel better.

SAVE 5,000 STEPS

Here is another thought to save you time and energy. Instead of hanging hubby's pajamas in the closet, try placing them under his pillow. Do the same for your nightgown. This eliminates about fourteen steps a day. Figure it out . . . seven to the closet and seven back! Multiply that by 365 days a year and see how many steps you will save in the years you expect to live! This is most convenient in more ways than one. Your husband can't say, "Where are my pajamas?" or "I can't find my pajamas." And you haven't wasted 5,000 steps a year.

GIVE PILLOWS THE AIR

Pillows are an important factor for good sleeping and proper rest. They should be aired or tumbled in a dryer (without heat, of course) to be soft and fluffy. This eliminates turning and complaining from your husband because they are knotty. (The heat and oil from our skin causes feather pillows to pack.)

When a pillow is aired on the clothes line, turn it upside down about three times and fluff it each time. Never leave pillows in the strong sun too long as it dries out the natural oil in the feathers. The fresh smell from the sunshine will give "papa" the best sleep he has ever had. You will love the fresh fluffy pillows, too.

CUT DOWN ON SWEEPING

I wouldn't tell you this if I thought it wasn't worth every little bit of energy you will save. . . . It is not necessary to sweep under your beds every day. Who is going to look under

your beds? Save your energy . . . never waste it. Cleaning under beds once a week is considered good housekeeping nowadays. Especially since most people have carpets. And if you don't, so what?

BRIGHTEN UP THE BATHROOM

Now begin with the bathroom and see how long it takes to clean it and if you can make it more attractive.

Bare walls? Cold-looking? Remedy it.

I bet that you have darling baby pictures tucked away in some old book that no one ever sees! It is not considered good taste today to put ten pictures on your dresser and about five on each table. Besides, it makes houses harder to keep clean.

Get the pictures out of the desk drawer. Dime-store frames are in order. The plain little black ones cost only about thirty cents. Put your baby pictures in them! Hang a big one or a group of small ones in your bathroom.

Odd? Yes, but be different. You will get so much pleasure looking at them each time you go in to take a shower. And your friends and house guests will enjoy them, too.

Buy colored bath towels. They will lend eye-spice to decoration. They are easier to launder than white, and smudges and dirt stains don't show on them so easily.

Carpets? Absolutely! This may sound odd but you will save yourself the time and energy required to wax floors (to say nothing of the cost of the wax), daily sweeping and washing bathmats.

Look for a cotton run on sale. Once in a while you can get a real bargain. Any woman can carpet her own floor. One nine-by-twelve rug will usually cover two bathrooms and a dressing room. If you only have one bathroom, either buy a small rug or get one of your friends to split one with you.

If you have wooden moldings on floors, buy colored carpet tacks to match and tack the rug to the bottom of the baseboard or directly into the floor itself.

Save the scraps! Cut little pieces to use as small bathmats.

Instead of waxing and mopping, use your carpet sweeper to clean your bathroom floor. You will find it won't need sweeping as often as you thought it would. Gives you a feeling of luxury, too.

Now, about washing the tub. Use your broom to do this. Wet the tub and sprinkle cleanser in it. Let the water faucet drip slowly and your old kitchen broom will do the rest for you without your having to stoop over.

No need to buy bathtub brushes and mops. Mops need to be wrung out and this is only an unnecessary chore. By using the broom you have accomplished two things with one stroke. You have also washed your broom! How long has it been since you washed your broom? A broom needs washing after you have swept your floor with it repeatedly. Keep it clean. Protect your carpets. Another good way to clean your broom is to pour some ammonia into a pail of water and swish the broom around in it and rinse. Wait until you see how dirty your broom was!

There are many products on the market to clean the basin and chrome. But to save money and energy and to get the best shine possible, use an old wash cloth slightly dunked in kerosene. Your chrome will shine like new! Kerosene removes scum from the fixtures, including the outside of the toilet bowl. The kerosene odor leaves in a few minutes. Once again, be careful in using kerosene—it's flammable and it should be stored outside the house—in a garage or shed.

If you don't like kerosene, use rubbing alcohol. Take a piece of toilet tissue and pour alcohol on it. Rub the mirror first. You will be surprised how clean it gets. Next, wipe the wash basin. Then the toilet fixtures. Presto—the bathroom is clean! Alcohol is cheap, it removes soap film and it leaves no water spots. But best of all, it is usually kept in the bathroom cabinet.

Clean that bathroom cabinet today. It takes only a few minutes. Discard all old medicines; they are dangerous. And did you know that all medicine should be dated? So simple.

KEEP KITCHEN PAINTED

Is your kitchen worn in spots? Especially where the handles and knobs are on the cupboards and drawers? No amount of cleaning is going to make it look better!

My kitchen has just had its fourth coat of paint in two years. Know why? Mainly because I test everything that people recommend for washing woodwork and swear it won't remove the paint! But it does. . . . Before you use a woodwork cleaner (even if it is guaranteed) test it! No use taking all the paint off the entire kitchen.

Use a dark piece of terry cloth (like a wash rag or other soft cloth) and apply your favorite cleanser. Then see if the paint shows on the cloth. If it does, you are removing the paint. Also, wait a few hours and see if the spot you washed is dull. If so, you have removed the gloss, too.

I just painted my kitchen. I did it myself this time. I *know* what kind of paint it has on it. It's beautiful and shiny. Never buy cheap paint for the kitchen. We wash it so often that this is where we need the best brand that we can afford.

Besides, expensive paint goes farther and is cheaper in the long run.

PUT ON A SHOW FOR HIM!

A word of caution: buy the best paint brush you can afford. This saves streaks and makes the paint smooth. Clean the brush afterwards. For ten cents you can get paint-brush cleaners at your hardware and dime stores. Paint brushes can be used for years if they are properly taken care of.

If you have never painted before, don't try inside painting. This means the inside of the cabinets. Paint only the outside of the cabinets. One coat of paint usually takes one quart of paint and one quart of turpentine. You will need the latter for thinning and cleaning up spatters. You will also use it for cleaning the paint off your hands and shoes.

By limiting yourself to outside painting you will have the job done in a few hours. This is best done when your husband is home. Why? If he won't help you at least he can see how hard you have worked!

Place papers all over the floor first, *then* start washing the woodwork. This must be done. Kitchens have grease fumes and spatters and oily marks on doors from our hands. No paint will stick when applied over oil. I used tri-sodium phosphate to wash the woodwork and found it excellent. It was easy to use and it removed film and dirt.

You will find that your sponge will be filled with paint as you rinse from one spot to the next. Rinse your sponge out often. I made my solution extra strong as I wanted to remove the top greasy paint.

Your husband can wash and you paint. (This saves *your* hands!) Also ask your husband to remove the hardware. Tell him you don't know how!

Never let your paint get too thick. If you do, it will leave streaks. If you find it getting thick and your brush is hard to "pull," then thin it. Two thin coats are easier to apply and look much better than one thick coat, anyway.

If you apply a second coat (next day, after you have rested) make the paint thinner and it will go on twice as fast as the first coat did. This will remove all marks and cover any mistakes you made the first time. It did mine.

Why not have a beautiful kitchen? Paint it today.

Think! You spend most of your time in your kitchen. Enjoy it! If a kitchen is in need of paint, it's depressing. Why be depressed when, for a few dollars, you can enjoy the beauty of a clean, shiny new kitchen?

WATCH THAT WAX!

A woman sent the following piece of advice: "Tell people to be very careful about putting some wax-type cleaners on their kitchen woodwork. We had a terrible experience after using some. When the painter repainted our woodwork, he followed his usual procedure of removing the surface dirt, but this did not reach all the built-up wax and later the paint started to peel. We had to use paint remover and take every door and drawer right down to the bare wood. The painter advised us to use any wax sparingly!"

SPARE THE ELBOW GREASE!

I have just learned how to clean a dirty, greasy stove without elbow grease or expensive bottled stuff that you must go out and buy.

The main thing I hate about cleaning an oven is using steel-wool pads that always ruin fingernails and still do not get into the corners! Recently a home economist was in my home. At the time she mentioned that after we broil steaks, we should rinse, dampen, then sprinkle granulated detergent on the used broiler and let it stand. The burnt grease would come right off. She was right . . . it did.

Now . . . with all the baking we do and the pies and meats

that run over onto the shelves . . . the stove begins looking terrible. I have tried many products to remove these crusty, burned, brown spots on both the oven and the stove. But I can never get the grills clean without losing a fingernail and my temper. I decided that I would try using detergent on all the removable parts of the oven and leave them overnight.

I used my washtub, filled it to the brim with hot water and added two cups of detergent. (You can use your bathtub at night if your sink isn't big enough and you have no washtub.) I took all of the grills, racks, pans, bottom of the oven (everything that would come loose) and put them under the hot water. I left them overnight to see what would happen.

Next morning, I picked up one of the oven racks and, lo and behold, if it wasn't clean! Only little particles of apple pie were left. With a vegetable brush they quickly rubbed off. I have never had such a clean oven and stove. The grease and burned particles floated to the top of the water. Amazing!

Now . . . let me give you one word of advice on this. I do not recommend doing it in the daytime. You may need the oven before the articles are clean. I suggest that you put all of these things in to soak after you do your dinner dishes. This way you will not need your oven again that day. In the morning, even though you are in a hurry to cook breakfast and need your oven, you will have no trouble as there will be nothing left to do but rinse off the parts you need and replace them. Wait until after breakfast when the family has gone before replacing the rest of the parts.

Now . . . aren't you just dying to clean that oven and stove? What a wonderful feeling it will be to see them shine with no effort, no broken fingernails and no wasted energy. Take a nap with that time saved.

GETTING RID OF TILE FILM

Bathroom ceramic tile film can be removed. Use plain, dry, fine steel wool (and not the soapy kind) and a *completely* dry shower. It is very important that both the steel wool and the tile be completely dry before attempting to remove tile film. Just take a dry piece of fine steel wool and scour the tile. The dirty scum will come off like talcum powder! This may be washed down the drain afterwards. I suggest that you cover your head to protect your hair from the powder. Do not use this on export tile or other kinds. *Test* first before doing the whole bath.

And, ladies, once the film is off . . . keep it off! Suggestions are: kerosene (just dip an old cloth in kerosene and wipe the walls about once a week); paste waxes (just wax the walls once they are dry). Some people even use furniture polish. I can't say positively, but I believe this film is caused by soap spatters. I have found that most of it is eliminated if some sort of protection is put on the tiles after cleaning.

I suggest that none of these methods be used on the floor of the shower as this causes it to be slippery. Apply any of the methods *only* to the walls where the tile is.

I'M FOR PLASTIC PAILS!

To me, plastic wastebaskets and garbage pails are among the most wonderful inventions man ever made. No rust or corrosion, and they seem to outlast the older types.

I have found that they do get dirty, though. Naturally, unless you are a perfectionist, you don't clean them daily.

If you have a washing machine with the hose that drains into the wash tub, set your garbage pails and wastebaskets under the hose as you do your laundry! The hot soapy water that drains from your washing machine will fill the garbage pail and get it clean. The rinse water will rinse it. Result— clean garbage pails and no effort.

Those of you who don't have laundry baskets, use the clean pail to take each load of laundry to the line. This saves many trips. For each load of laundry that you do, put another dirty pail under the hose—kitchen pail, bathroom pail, living room wastebaskets, and so on until all of your wastebaskets are clean. Who said laziness wasn't the mother of invention? I'm learning.

MAKE A STOCKING MOP

A Scotsman passed this tip along: "All women just hate to wash a floor mop. They sour and can accumulate more seemingly impossible dirt that you can't get out. I made my wife the grandest mop from about twenty of her old discarded nylon stockings. I cut the tops and feet off the stockings and knotted them together in the center of each length.

"My wife says that she has never enjoyed a mop more as it doesn't sour, it is easily washed and, most of all . . . it's so easy for her to wring. The nylon is lightweight (which she swears helps her aching back) and doesn't leave streaks on her floor. Nor do strings catch on the furniture.

"As it cost nothing to make one, others might try it. I cannot seem to see for the life of me why someone hasn't manufactured one on this order. But for the price my wife spends on stockings each month, a mop of this order probably would break a man's budget!"

NEWSPRINT'S GREAT FOR WINDOWS

We all have windows. They *do* get dirty. No doubt about it. Our problem is to find the easiest way to wash them. Over the last three years I have tried every method that has been sent in. I have twenty-three big windows in my home, plus glass sliding doors.

Plain ol' rubbing alcohol will remove fly specks easily when applied with a facial tissue.

For washing, I crumple up a few newspapers and dip them in water and wring them out just as if I were using a rag. There is something in printer's ink used on newsprint paper that makes glass shine. This will not work if magazines are used. It must be a soft paper.

When you're left with a streak on the windows . . . and don't know which side the streak is on . . . I have found that the answer is to wash and polish the inside windows with an up-and-down motion. Polish all outside windows crossways.

If the result leaves a streak, then you know if it is on the inside or outside by the direction the streak runs!

I also find that by tearing one sheet of newspaper in half, I have a perfect size to work with. Carry a bowl of warm water and vinegar solution with you as you work . . . you can dip a new piece of newspaper into the solution once it gets dirty.

A chamois is the next best thing and for some windows it's even better. Many people like this. I have used it and find it wonderful. I cannot tell much difference in cheap and expensive chamois. Buy these at your dime store or your filling station. They are wonderful for mirrors and glass table tops.

And, gals, you and I both know that your windows won't stay clean unless your screens are clean. Screens collect dust. The rain and wind come along and scatter the dust that has collected on your screens onto your windows. I cannot see washing windows without washing screens, too.

People have sent me many tips on washing windows. A sampling follows:

TRY A SQUEEGEE

"First thing one should do is invest in a window squeegee. This can be bought at any department or hardware store. Then buy a sponge. Reserve this sponge for washing windows *only*. Rinse this sponge thoroughly after each window washing job.

"When washing windows, I use about one-half cup of non-sudsing ammonia to a gallon of hot water. Dip sponge into this and wash window, rinse sponge and go over the window again to get any spots that you might have missed.

"Next, use squeegee, going across the window until the width of the window is wiped. Bring the squeegee down the side of the glass to finish. Use a clean rag to wipe the squeegee after each stroke. Then wipe the edge of the window with the rag to pick up any water drops.

"*Never* wash windows when the sun is shining on them as this will cause streaks and result in a very poor job."

Note: I tried this method. It's fantastic. I didn't have a squeegee so I took a windshield wiper from the car! Wonderful! Suggest that people save their old windshield wipers. They are great.

VINEGAR CUTS THE DIRT

From Pennsylvania: "Our windows were terrible from being water-spotted on the outside after we watered the lawn. (We

have hard water.) We tried everything from soap pads to cleansers to remove the spots. Nothing helped. My husband then used pure vinegar on a cloth and rubbed the glass hard. The water spots disappeared and the windows looked shiny and new again. They didn't even streak. I suggest if people are just washing soiled windows that they put vinegar in the water mixture they ordinarily use!"

SPRAY SUGGESTION

From Massachusetts: "A pharmacist gave me a wonderful window-washing suggestion: Get a bottle of rubbing alcohol that will fit a bottle sprayer (with extension). Have the pharmacist add a few drops of straight ammonia (which is stronger than household ammonia) and you will have a wonderful spray which will cut grease and dirt . . . yet will not streak as it contains no water. I especially like this for big windows and mirrors because one can do them in sections without leaving division streaks."

QUICK TRICKS

To remove wax from the felt pads of a floor polisher, place the pads between several thicknesses of paper towels and press with a warm iron . . . the old wax will absorb on the paper towels in a matter of seconds.

Here's an excellent idea for stainless steel: Wash with detergent as usual. Then apply a little mineral oil on a soft cloth. Wipe off the excess and *voilà!* It's a miracle.

Two pieces of paper toweling make an excellent dust cloth. Wet hands and dry on two sections of paper towel. Apply a little furniture polish on one towel and polish. Buff with the other one! Then discard. No dirty cloths lying around!

After years of throwing a dust cloth over the end of a broom to clean cobwebs off walls and ceilings, someone told me of a new and easier method. I now save all the old socks, slip one or two over the end of a yardstick and secure them with a rubber band. This is not nearly as tiring as holding a heavy broom, and you can get into much smaller spaces. This same sock over the yardstick is good for cleaning under the refrigerator and other pieces of furniture that are close to the floor.

To clean those delicate, intricate designs on silver pieces, where you must get into the little tiny cracks . . . use a mascara brush! Wonderful for the little filigree charms on your bracelet. The brush will get into the tiniest crevices.

Silver will be bright and shiny if washed in very hot soapy water and dried as if you were polishing it. The secret of shiny silver is in the drying.

To keep bathroom walls and ceiling clean and shiny, wipe them with a clean rag right after a steamy bath. If you keep the windows and doors of the bathroom shut during the bath or shower the walls will be quite moist and may be wiped clean with a minimum of strain. Mildew is checked, too. Use a sponge mop with a new refill for reaching the upper parts of the walls and ceiling.

Buy a rubber tip (the kind that fits on crutches and kitchen stool legs) from a dime store and put it on the top of your broom handle. It's grand. It keeps the broom from marking the wall when resting against it, and if you turn it upside down to put in the closet, it doesn't fall.

A mitten made from an old towel, oval in shape, with elastic run through the hem near the wrist, can be worn on one hand while doing your cleaning. It is a terrific dust rag and can be put in the regular laundry.

A simple way of getting dust off waxed kitchen floors: Put two paper towels on the floor and place the dust mop on top of them and mop. You will be surprised what adheres to those towels. And it sure keeps a clean mop!

If you dampen the inside of your dustpan under the faucet before picking up the little pile of dust and dirt, the dust sticks to the pan. No sneezing!

A woman from Rhode Island sent this tip: "I rub my aluminum screens and doors with a cloth that has been dipped in kerosene and then wipe them off. This has kept them from pitting. If this is done about twice a year when they are still new, pitting can be prevented."

LOOK FOR REFRIGERATOR DUST

A woman from California sent this tip: "I disconnected my refrigerator and removed the bottom panel. When I looked under it and saw the dust and lint on the motor, I was amazed. We had been having trouble with it and were going to call the repairman. When I plugged the refrigerator back in after cleaning, it worked like new again. It's a good idea to clean this part of the refrigerator once a month."

BURN THE SKILLET CLEAN

The best way to clean an iron skillet that over the years has acquired a thick coating of grease on the outside and some on the inside is to find someone who has a coal furnace. Throw the skillet into any furnace for half an hour on the hot coals and presto . . . it comes out brand new again. Coal stoves and outdoor grills will help, too. All that is required is heat—to burn off the stale grease.

One woman passed along a hint on preventing rust in iron skillets: "When the skillet is clean and ready to be put away, wad a bit of wax paper, dipped in an odorless salad oil, and rub this into the skillet thoroughly. When the skillet is thus 'seasoned,' it is much easier to clean. The same rule applies to all metalized utensils, even those aboard a boat or in a summer cabin. Salt air and general dampness can't get through the coating of oil and if this procedure is used, things will never need a harsh scrubbing."

A woman from Georgia wrote: "The wooden handle on my skillet has become charred where it fits into the metal, and turns. Do you know if it is possible to get replacement handles and if so where?"

This was my reply: Look at the bottom of your skillet and you will probably see a brand name. Call some store that carries this same brand of merchandise. They will give you the address of the company. Write to the company and they will send all information, prices, etc. Don't ever use a pot or pan with a loose handle. Each year hundreds of people are badly burned when they pick up something and the handle either falls off or turns.

REACH FOR THE SALT

When something spills or cooks over in your oven—just sprinkle salt immediately. When the oven is cool, use your pancake turner and pick up the burned pile of "goop." Wipe with damp sponge. Terrific!

I had scalloped potatoes boil over yesterday . . . and what smoke and smell. I immediately grabbed my box of salt and poured it on the burned spills. Smoke died down, odors left, and I just kept cooking. After removing the food, I closed the oven door so the heat would stay in the oven. Next morning, I just used my pancake turner and scraped up the awful mess.

I suggest that women should not try to clean a mess like this when it happens. Close the oven door and let the heat finish your chores! There is always tomorrow!

TRY A POTATO DIP ON PANS

Dip a raw potato into scouring powder to scrub the corners of rusted cake and pie pans.

KEEP TOASTER CLEAN

A Texas woman sent this: "I wonder how many people know that there is a hinged tray on the bottom of many toasters for cleaning purposes? I didn't until yesterday. When my friend told me this, I went right home and opened it and it was loaded with grease and crumbs. Here's the way to clean it: Scrape most of the grease off with a spatula and then take a feather from your duster and carefully wipe the insides. Don't use a knife for this as the parts are very delicate. *Be sure to unplug the toaster before you clean it.*"

3.

Coping with the Kids

~~~~~~

"APPETEASERS"

Try putting a large dish of carrot and celery sticks in front of the children just before dinner while they are watching TV. This keeps them from dipping into the pots on the stove, the bread box or the refrigerator and doesn't dull their appetites. You won't fret later if they don't eat all their vegetables.

LUNCH TREAT

For children's lunch boxes: Try packing vegetable and fruit salads in small jars or containers. The salads are often left over from the previous night's dinner and they're a nice change from sandwiches.

NO MORE MIX-UPS

A young mother sent me the following hint: "I bought some of those colored ink markers at the dime store. I find these invaluable for keeping track of my children's clothing. I bought five colors and each child marks his own clothes with a dot of his particular color. When sorting the laundry, I now just look for that dot of color on socks, underwear, and their belongings, and pile all of one color together. I also put a corresponding color inside each child's drawer. When the drawer is opened the dot on the clothes matches the dot on the inside of the drawer. This way the children's clothes don't get mixed up and they can find their own."

Why don't you start a new fad and have kids wear unmated socks? I'll bet it would spread like wildfire among the teen-agers. Sure would take care of the odd socks around the house.

KEEP 'EM ANCHORED

To keep small children from throwing toothbrushes down the drain . . . tie each toothbrush onto the toothbrush holder with a piece of twine long enough to permit children to brush their teeth. It's not fancy, but it is practical.

A SHIRT TALE

For kids who hate to wear bibs and aprons at home or school when eating or painting: cut the collar off of Dad's old white shirt. This will look sort of like an artist's smock. Put the shirt on the child backward so the buttons will be in the back. No little boy seems to mind this much . . . when it's Dad's! It covers completely.

DO-IT-YOURSELF TOYS

A woman told me that her grandchildren discovered her stack of empty milk cartons one day (she uses them for storing leftovers in the refrigerator). The kiddies had a grand time building houses and all sorts of things with them! Others have written that these boxes can have holes punched in them at the top and bottom. Give a child a long string to "thread" the boxes to form a train! For rainy days, this is something quite different and the cost is nothing. It keeps the child occupied and out of mother's hair while she makes her phone calls and does her housework.

Also, if you give the child a pair of school scissors (blunt points), he can spend hours cutting the cartons and creating airplanes, trucks (by using empty spools from thread as wheels) and little girls can make doll beds, cradles and all kinds of furniture. Lollipop sticks can be used to create many things with these boxes.

After the youngsters are through with their "mess," the cartons can be discarded. Oatmeal and salt boxes are wonderful, too. Cereal boxes (small size) are another thing that is terrific for little children. They can be colored or pasted together. Colored paper may be glued, taped or stapled to them.

Let your child literally mess up one room today! But . . . tell him that he *must* clean up everything all by himself when he is finished.

THE VERSATILE TV TRAY

Those TV trays have another use. When children use paints . . . set up two trays for each child, side by side. On one tray put the child's drawing paper and on the other tray put his paints. Put newspapers on the floor beneath both trays. This prevents spills on the floor. When the child is through messing, just dump all the mess onto the newspaper that's on the floor. Then roll it up and discard. What a lifesaver for mother! When weather permits, let the children paint in the yard or on the porch. Even the garage is a good place. If there is no garage, for some people the kitchen is wonderful.

HAIR CARE

An easy way to cut daughter's bangs evenly is to dampen them slightly with a comb. While still damp, tear off a piece of cellulose tape and place it over the bangs . . . across the forehead, exactly where you want to cut them. You can then snip (with the scissors) across the *top* of the tape and will have a perfectly straight line. This also keeps the hair from falling in the child's face.

Did you know that you could take peanut butter and rub it in a child's hair and it will remove chewing gum? It does work! Just put a dab of it on the hair and rub gently between your fingers. The peanut butter will loosen the gum. Pick this up with a cleaning tissue or toilet tissue. It's far better than cutting a child's hair and having a "chunk" out! Wash hair as usual.

You can tackle the problem of washing children's hair by using the "drainboard-brush" method.

Put the child on her back on the kitchen drainboard (on a few bath towels) and put her head over the sink with a sponge under her neck. After applying shampoo, use a hair brush to wash the hair with until clean. With a spray attached to the faucet, the job is complete. If you cannot afford a spray, rinsing can be done with a basin of water and a cup.

Children rebel against shampoos because they are afraid of getting soap in their eyes. This method eliminates this problem as the child is face-up and can see and talk to mother.

NO MORE LOST LACES

A helpful hint for mothers who have small children who like to untie their shoes and unlace them: Tie a small knot at the *end* of each shoestring after lacing the shoe . . . the child can still remove the shoes, but not the laces.

CHOP YOUR FOOD BUDGET

When young children are in the chopped food stage, you can save from three to five dollars a week by making it yourself! The food chopper or blender is well worth anyone's money. A food chopper costs about three dollars. Blenders are a little more but will pay for themselves within a month or so when used for this purpose alone!

I also think mothers make better tasting food for the little ones by making it themselves. When using nutritious and inexpensive meats to make stews for the family, what is left can go into the blender for the baby. After using a food chopper, these items can be pressed through a food masher (which costs about a dollar) if a blender is too much for the budget.

If fruits and vegetables are desired they can be prepared in the same manner and will keep about four days in the refrigerator. Be sure to cap the containers well.

PIN UP TOWELS

Here's a hint for mothers whose little children invariably leave the towel on the bathroom floor instead of hanging it up. Take two or three safety pins, drape one edge of the towel over the towel rack and pin the edge of the towel, leaving enough hanging down so the youngest child can reach it.

SAVE THOSE SIX-PACKS

Here is an easy way to handle or store baby bottles in or out of the refrigerator. Save the cardboard carrying cartons that hold the six-pack drink bottles. When making formula, lift the filled bottles from the sterilizer and put them in the carton. Place in refrigerator. This carton can be moved about so that anything that is stored in back of it can be reached easily.

MAKE A BOTTLE HOLDER

A hint for mothers with babies who drink milk from glass bottles, and find the bottles are slick and often dropped: Use a cotton stocking to cover the bottle! The stocking is soft and the baby's hands cling to it . . . and he learns to hold his own bottle faster! Also . . . after a child reaches a certain age, he tends to drop and break his bottle, which leaves a mother with the task of picking up broken glass. The stocking eliminates that problem, too.

WHY BE A DIAPER DRUDGE?

Diapers are diapers and they are here to stay as long as there are babies! It seems as if all mothers do is take them off, put them on, wash them again and fold . . . then start over! It is absolutely endless. Economy of motion is the only way to save energy on diaper drudgery.

Soak them in a pail of cold water with a little pine disinfectant added. This elminates all odors. Empty the entire pail into the washing machine and let the solution spin dry, then wash as usual through the entire cycle.

Shake diapers before hanging them on the line. Try hanging them two at a time. This saves clothespins, time and energy. When a mother can do something with half the effort she should certainly take advantage of it!

For mothers who have those dull baby-diaper pins: take a bar of pure baby soap (it's softer and doesn't crumble as badly as some others), leave the wrapper on the bar and stick your pins into the soap. Pins will go through the diaper ever so easily and the wrapper will keep any little bits that might flake in one container. Later, this same bar can be used to bathe baby. Another method is: Run the tip of the pin through your hair before pinning the diaper. Seems silly, but it works!

Another tip on diapers: As soon as junior is big enough (about 20 pounds), fold all his diapers and sit down at the machine and sew them. Result? No more boring diaper folding. They wash and dry just as easily as before.

All children like to throw things . . . just anything. So why not make bean-bags out of leftover cloth materials? Make them about four or six inches square and don't fill them with too many beans. They're wonderful rainy day sport for the kiddies; they can be played with in the basement and thrown hard . . . yet no one gets hurt.

SIMPLIFIED BEDMAKING

Want to teach your young daughter to make her own bed? Sew a colored string to the center of each blanket, sheet and bed spread so that she can find the center of each and line them all up properly. Then put a colored mark or thumbtack on the center of the headboard as a guide. Now . . . she can learn to make her own bed beautifully all by herself!

THE NAME-TAPE PROBLEM

A tip from a mother: "Instead of adhesive or name tapes for rainwear I wrote my son's name with a dry ink marker right on the inside of his raincoat and hat. I also wrote his first name (on the outside at the back) on his left boot and his last name on the right boot. This not only solved the name-tape problem but my son knows if he stands the boots in front of him and can read his name properly . . . each boot will be on the proper foot! These ink markers are wonderful for many things, such as marking toys, books, lunch pails and all school equipment and yard tools."

FOR STICKY LITTLE HANDS

Here's a goodie: When going on a picnic with children, take wet wash cloths, fold each in a small square, and put them in sandwich bags. Then put them in your picnic bag. The wax paper bags will prevent the dampness from contacting other things. Also, fold a dry wash cloth or two into another wax paper sack and have these for drying.

IT'S A SMALL WORLD

For mothers who have trouble getting little children to eat: These are *little* people and this should be remembered. Give them eating utensils according to their size. Serve their meals on little salad or butter plates. How would you like to eat off a turkey platter each night? That is the way they feel. The big plate is overwhelming for a small child.

Dig out those unused butter spreaders. They are blunt and small and just right for the little ones to spread their peanut butter and jelly.

Let a child eat with a salad fork! It is much wider and shorter than a dinner fork and much easier for him to handle.

Serve hot soup and cold milk in coffee mugs with handles. These are much easier for children to grasp and this avoids "slopping" soup and spilling or turning over milk glasses.

Most mothers will find that little children will begin to eat more if this method is used. And remember, little children love a miniature world. That is why they love "little" things like dolls, animals, chairs and tables. So why not apply it to eating? It has worked in many families with picky eaters.

IN BRIEF . . .

You can solve the problem of too-thin diapers for children who wet at night by using old flannel receiving blankets.

If small children open the lower cabinets of your cupboards, invest in a pair of dime-store toy handcuffs . . . cut in two the chain that connects them and use one handcuff to lock each handle on the cabinet door. These can be removed in a second by you, but the child cannot manipulate them. Sure saves mother lots of time picking up her pots and pans.

Here's a handy timesaving hint for mothers with grade-school boys: Buy shirts with the sleeves too long, turn the cuff of each up at the seam and change the button to the other side of the cuff. This makes it look like a French cuff with a cuff link. When the cuff is ironed up this way, it will stay flat and neat. This method allows for growing, as the cuff can be turned down later on and the shirt worn much longer.

For mothers of young babies who do not like the plastic bibs: Take one of those little fingertip towels with fringe on the ends, and cut into it. Shape a neck and bind with bias tape. The bib can go right into the laundry, and no ironing is required.

Some teachers ask mothers to put loops on children's jackets for easy hanging. A strip of narrow elastic about two inches long will have enough "give" to enable several items to be hung on one hook.

Keep a white sock in your bathroom and put all small pieces of soap into it. Tie a knot at the open end of the sock and use this at bathtime for kiddies. Very handy, and they love it—something different.

When children's shoes are scuffed badly and don't seem to take polish, simply rub them with a piece of raw potato and then apply the polish. They will shine like new.

Blankets that a child has outgrown should not be discarded. They can be sewn on three sides to form a "sack" for the baby to sleep in! These little sacks keep the baby's feet warm and not only are a saving but are very convenient.

You can warm baby's food in an egg poacher. Fill the bottom with warm water and put different foods in each compartment. This saves lots of dirty dishes. The aluminum heats faster than regular china baby plates, too.

4.

Away with Washday Woes!

~~~~~~

If today is your washday . . . let's make that chore fun! Don't just wash. Let's wash and accomplish something. How? Get the thrill and satisfaction of seeing your clothes snowy white.

This is not an approved method written by any authority. I am no authority. This is my own method which I experimented with and found successful. Many have tried it and found it "the lazy woman's way" to beautiful laundry which makes any woman proud.

Gather up all of your *white* clothes. (This does not refer to some new synthetics which do not take to *hot* water.) Put them in your washing machine. Set the water on "hot." Be sure that you have lots of hot water in your tank.

Do not overload your machine. Let's underload it today. Add bleach and detergent to the hot water.

After your washing machine has been running about two minutes and you are sure that the soap is well mixed among the clothes with the bleach . . . turn the machine off—then let the clothes stand ten minutes. After this period the dirt starts clinging to the fibers again—no matter what brand of soap you use. So do not let it stand longer than ten minutes. If you cannot turn your machine off manually, pull out the electric plug. Do not turn any dials. You will want the complete cycle to run its course. After ten minutes, turn the machine back on and let it go!

This method saves individual bleaching, and avoids possible rotting of your clothes by not using too much bleach each time. Also, we usually bleach two or three articles each week and then what do we do? Put them right back in with other soap-filmed clothes! Don't do this. Bleach all of your clothes at one time; wash them together and they will not accumulate the "film" that causes dirty, yellow clothes and depressing washdays.

These clothes are now practically, but not *completely*, soap-free. For those of you who want to do a thorough job, follow this second step:

Run the same load of clothes through the entire cycle again, this time using a water softener or vinegar and *no* soap. I use vinegar because it is cheaper and really . . . we all have it in our homes. This will brighten your clothes by removing remaining soap film. It will also remove the "gray" from your dark clothes and brighten your colored ones. When I use vinegar, I put in about a cup to a machine load of clothes.

Another way to put the gray right back into your clothes is to use too much soap. Test your particular machine. The water varies in different localities. "Feel" the water that you are washing your clothes in. If the water is "soft" when you rub your fingers together in it and your fingers "slip," then you have enough soap!

SPARE THE SOAP!

Try cutting your amount of soap in half! Overuse of soap is a common mistake among many homemakers. They think the more soap they use, the cleaner the wash. Not so! Too much soap causes soap film. If you cut the amount of soap in half and the water is still slippery, then you have been using too much soap.

Most people want to know, "How do I save?" Soap is expensive, so why waste it? You wouldn't think of throwing an extra cup of sugar down the drain when you bake a cake. Yet you actually not only throw half of your detergent away when you do your laundry, but you use *extra* bleach to remove it!

Do not waste the bleach, either. Why rot the clothes and the elastic in garments? Once you have removed the soap film from your clothes and they are white, they will be easy to keep that way.

Remember . . . never overload your machine.

Now that you have read this, go gather the white clothes out of your laundry and put them in your washing machine.

You must have hot water. Always rinse in hot water to get extremely white clothes. Some machines automatically rinse in cold water. Until your clothes reach "perfection" . . . use and set your dial for rinsing on hot water.

Wait a while before starting that second load of clothes, to give the heater time to recover the high heat that you will need.

For colored clothes, leave out bleach but add one-fourth cup of ammonia with your detergent. Go through the same procedure and use vinegar rinse.

After clothes are soap-free, one-fourth cup of vinegar will do.

If your clothes are not white on washday, try these hints. The first thing to do is get your clothes white. The second thing is to keep them that way!

OVERLOADING—A COMMON FAULT

The most common fault, I found with my experiments, was overloading the washing machine. Naturally, clothes cannot "swish" around if there are too many of them in the washer.

You may have a ten-pound capacity washer (some machines have only eight pounds) but you probably have no way to weigh the clothes. The way to test this is to fill your washing machine with water first (on top loaders) and then put your clothes in.

After the agitator starts, look in the machine to see if your clothes are "swishing" around and turning freely. If your clothes do not change position immediately, you have overloaded your machine and your clothes will never get really clean. Take some of the clothes out. Eventually, you will be able to judge without going through this procedure.

RINSE 'EM RIGHT SMART

Improper rinsing is the main cause of gray and yellow clothes. When clothes have soap remaining in them, they cannot possibly get white. This soap builds up and eventually causes soap *film*.

As soon as any heat (electric iron or body heat) touches clothes that have soap left in them . . . they will turn dirty gray or yellow! They will scorch more easily, too. The soap also rots fabrics and wears out clothes.

Test your machine by watching your drain hose (where the water comes out). Some machines rinse only once. After the wash cycle, let the machine spin dry.

If your machine is one that only rinses once (or is a manual washer and you have been rinsing your clothes only once), put a small amount of water in the clothes again . . . now . . . when this spins dry, just look at the water hose again and if the water is clouded and not clear, you have been rinsing your clothes in partially soapy water!

In the final rinse, add water softener. One-half cup of vinegar will do the same thing. I use vinegar as it is much cheaper. Watch for more suds as you run your machine through the complete cycle again.

If the water is still milky . . . this is soap film! It most likely has been there for a long time. After you get rid of this film, you probably will not have to use water softeners or vinegar.

Just don't get more soap film by using too much soap. Remember . . . try using half as much soap as you ordinarily have and see if your water is slippery; *never* soak clothes over ten minutes, and rinse *well!* Your clothes will get white and you will begin to enjoy laundering.

IF THERE WERE THIRTY-SIX HOURS IN A DAY . . .

I believe that even if the good Lord had given us mothers thirty-six hours in each day, and four hands, it would still not be enough to get all of our work done.

There isn't a mother in the world who hasn't wished that—just once—she could have all her laundry, ironing and grocery-buying done; the house cleaned, woodwork washed, tool shed cleaned out; rugs, draperies, upholstery and bedspreads washed.

We will never accomplish this. When we recognize this fact, we will get over some of those nervous and tired spells.

Until then, there is only one thing to do: Do what you can and *try* not to worry about the rest.

Remember, grandmother had to make her own soap and bread and scrub on a washboard! So if hubby says, "Why can't you?" look at him very sweetly and say, "Honey, why aren't you still driving a horse and buggy to work? Or maybe walking? Where is the pile of wood that you chopped tonight, and the milk from the cows?" So help me . . . men have reaped the rewards of modern inventions, but so have we.

What brought this topic up was a trip South. I am a firm believer that you learn from everyone.

As I watched a Southern washwoman hang up the clothes on her many lines, I felt sorry for her because she did not have a dryer. But she preferred the sun. She told me that the sun bleaches things. She put some very gray things on the green grass. I asked her why. "The grass bleaches, and my clothes are white," she said. I recalled that we put salt and lemon on things and laid them on the grass to bleach them.

Then . . . she took her garden hose, turned on the strongest stream of water, and hosed down the sheets, blue jeans, pillowcases, dish towels and all the flat work. She said this put weight in the fibers and *saved* ironing. She said she never hung a sheet by its tail, but across the line from the middle. (This way, the hems are on the bottom. The water drips, the wind blows and nature irons them!)

Later, when her clothes were dry, she started taking a few of them down off the line, leaving some . . . although they were dry, too.

She picked up the garden hose and casually started spraying

the clothes with the "fine spray." This was her easy way of "sprinkling." She did them all at once.

As she took them off the line she *folded* them and placed them in a basket. She said this prevented hard wrinkles! How smart! She never rolled them. That would make more wrinkles.

SATURDAY'S A GOOD WASH DAY

Did you know that Saturday is a good day to do your laundry? The children are home then and can help with it. Teach (notice I did not use the word "make") your children to help you hang up the clothes. Soon they will learn to separate them, too.

As they go along the clothesline, either holding the clothes or pinning them up (with your directions), you will find companionship with your children that you never had before. The children will actually enjoy helping. You will find that your laundry will not be burdensome but enjoyable because it will be shared.

After the clothes dry, ask the children or Daddy (this works too, because I tried it) to help you remove the clothes from the line. You unpin them and let the family hold them as you load the clothes into their arms. You will find that you can take the clothes down three times as fast.

Never let your family put their clothes in your ironing basket. Put a sheet on the floor in front of the TV! This is Saturday night and the entire family will be there. Leave the clothes there. I have a point here and will try to explain it.

Psychologically, all the clothes that members of the family

have used during the week will be in front of their noses. Whether they are aware of that fact or not . . . they will absorb it. They are proud of the stack of clean clothes.

Now, at TV intermission each person folds his own clothes and stacks them in piles. This can be done while the program is going on, too!

When the program is over, each person can take his clothes to his own room and place them in the proper drawers. This saves Mother hours of work on Mondays!

By the way, Mother, when you get to those sheets you will have help folding them. If you iron your sheets . . . iron them folded! They will still be full of the crisp air and if folded *now* before they "lie" too long, they will not have so many wrinkles in them and only the *top* of a sheet will need to be ironed. Did you know that? By Monday morning (if you fold them while still fresh from the line and before wrinkles form) the sheets will practically have ironed themselves. Put pillow slips on the bottom of the stack so the weight will press them flat.

As for Dad's pajamas and shorts (the children's, too) why iron them? Fold while still fresh and you won't have to.

The youngsters love to mate socks. Give them this job while you fold linen.

Never iron a dish towel. This is a waste of time. After you put laundry on the line (pinned correctly), take your garden hose and spray (I really wet mine thoroughly) all sheets, dish towels and flat work. The weight of the water will remove nearly every wrinkle! Big pieces, such as sheets, pillow slips and dish towels, can easily be folded as they come off the line.

A child's little wagon is a wonderful aid if you have no one to help you. Pull the wagon along under the clothesline as you remove the clothes and place them in it. Wagons are inexpensive and can be bought at many stores. These can be used for many things, too—yard work, carrying garbage cans and the like. For a few dollars spent on a small wagon you will save much in energy and backache.

STARCH IN YOUR WASHING MACHINE

Gals, if you have lots of starching to do . . . why don't you try it in your washing machine?

After the clothes have been washed and rinsed well . . . add a little water to the machine and pour in some strained, cooked laundry starch. Be sure to strain cooked starch through a fine tea strainer or cloth before pouring it into the machine (because sometimes it just isn't our day and it turns out lumpy!).

By setting the washing machine on about a three-minute cycle and letting the machine stir the clothes well, your starch will be evenly distributed throughout the clothes.

Many people (and I have found it works) use this method for a thin starching of entire garments.

I have found that you can save oodles of time if you use two different kinds of starch when doing laundry. Use the regular method first (as when you are starching shirts) and then as the garments are removed from the machine, you can use *permanent starch* on the collars, cuffs, and, if you like, down the front of the shirt.

By using two different kinds of starch when you first wash, you won't need to use the washing machine method for many times thereafter, as the permanent starches last through many washings.

Are the permanent starches worth the extra money we pay for them? I think so, when they're used for spot-starching.

Did you know that anything on your hands that is "slick," such as household washing bleach, can be removed by applying vinegar straight from the bottle, and then rinsing?

GET THAT GREASE!

For those of you troubled with "lines" on husband's shirt collars: Stop and think! Why is that line there? Why can't it be removed? What is keeping it in the shirt? Dirt? *No!* Dirt is on everything and it comes out in our washing. What does every man have? Oil? Grease? Yes!

How to remove them? With a grease and oil remover, of course.

It is a fact that any material (whether it be wool, cotton, linen, or whatever) which contains grease will accumulate dirt. Dust is in the air and, as the wind blows, it is bound to get on your husband's neck. This dust rubs off the natural oils which are in his neck and *sticks!*

Now . . . how to get rid of this? You *must* remove the oil before the dirt will come out.

Use an oil remover . . . or a grease or spot remover. Apply this to the neck of the shirt and let it sit awhile. Then the grease will dissolve . . . the dirt can't stick . . . and both will be gone when washed.

I have tried everything on the market for years. The most expensive is not always the best! I did find one product that cost a quarter that was wonderful . . . but since we are always looking for something cheaper and I do not like to mention brand names . . . I also found that dime-store chalk, which sells for about a dime, works wonders. Imagine! Something so simple.

Just mark along the neck with the chalk where the dirty, yellow line is (before washing), and if it's on the cuffs, mark along them, too. Let this sit for a while, at least an hour or so (overnight is even better). Then launder as usual. (Put it in your washing machine and use our laundry method.)

Mark heavily with the chalk. The chalk will absorb the oils and once the oils are removed . . . the dirt will come out! This requires no scrubbing, which usually wears out the collar.

One word of caution: This method may require a few applications if the yellow line has been there for years. If the shirt is a fairly new one, one application should remove it.

After removal of this line, as you do your laundry each week, take the chalk and mark across the collar. Then you shouldn't have this accumulation again. If the shirt is old and the line is stubborn, mark it with a heavy line of chalk, rub it in with your fingers and put it *back* in the laundry hamper. Let it sit until you do your laundry next time.

LAUNDERING NYLON

Nylon is a man-made fabric. Man-made fabrics have no "pores" because they come from a machine. These fabrics are quite different from "nature-made" fabrics.

Nylon, when washed with other clothes, *will* absorb the color from whatever you are washing! Home economists tell me this; I know it is so . . . but I can't tell you why or how! All I know is that if you put a white nylon blouse or shirt in the wash with anything colored, it will pick up the color of whatever you are washing with it!

If any garment has a tag on it that says "contains part nylon," then be careful about washing it with bath towels, housedresses or anything colored. White nylon should always be washed with other white things . . . or alone.

"BAG" YOUR SOCKS

An easy way to keep socks together when washing, to keep straps from wrapping themselves around everything in the washing machine, and to protect all lingerie, even nylons, is to put these "trouble-makers" in a bag made very simply of two dishcloths.

Buy the type of dishcloths that are made of loosely woven threads. Such cloths let plenty of suds and rinse water get inside. To make the bag, stitch two cloths together on three sides to look like a sack. It is usually best to stitch these sides several times so they will be secure. On the open side (or top of bag) stitch a hem about one inch deep. Turn the bag inside out so that the seams will be on the inside, and run a drawstring through the top. Your washing machine bag is finished, ready for months of service.

DON'T MIX 'EM!

From Virginia: "Hint that I learned from experience: never put a colored garment in with the white laundry! Takes too much bleach to fix (not to mention the teasing from the family when the underwear all comes out a beautiful pink)."

LET JEANS "PRESS" DRY

When washing blue jeans, pull the seams (inside and out) very hard before hanging them on the line. Pin the back of the pants with three clothespins on one line, pin the front of the pants on the next line, and they rarely need to be pressed.

UPSIDE DOWN'S BEST

When hanging shirts to dry, hang them upside down, with the two fronts lapped over each other. Pull on the side seams,

the two front seams and the sleeve seams. They dry beautifully and need practically no ironing.

STRINGS TANGLED?

For those who are plagued by apron strings that tangle
around clothes in the washer . . . try folding the strings a few
times and pinning them to the band of the apron with a
safety pin. Remove the pin when you hang the apron on the
line.

KILL TWO BIRDS—

For those who have badly stained dish towels that never
seem to come clean . . . soak all your dirty ones in the sink
with suds and bleach. Just let them sit awhile and see how
white they get. This will also bleach your sink and therefore
you get two jobs done at once.

THE SUN'S THE SECRET

From Pennsylvania: "I wondered about washing chicken
feather pillows . . . then I thought . . . I can wash feathers
and I can wash ticking, so I'll try it. A drowned cat looked
better than my pillows did when they came from the washing
machine! After the dryer they looked better but I was almost
in the market for new pillows. But after two days on the
clothesline in the sun, they puffed up to their natural softness
and they are now sweet-smelling and beautiful."

FRESHER CURTAINS

From Kentucky: "To renew the freshness and crispness of
nylon, dacron or fiber glass curtains . . . just add one-half cup
of powdered milk to the last rinse water. This will give them
body."

From Ohio: "To keep dacron curtains from looking limp,
I give mine a very light starching with instant starch and then
press them with a steam iron. This gives them a nice crispness
and avoids that 'tired' look."

ABOUT STARCHING . . .

From St. Louis: "I have found that when making your own spray starch, cooked starch is the best kind to use. I pour some of this in a bottle, add water to it, attach a spray top and spray away. The quart bottle can be kept in the refrigerator for refilling. The only drawback I've found is that the spray is not as fine as the commercially filled aerosol cans. My remedy for this is to put more distance between the sprayer and the fabric."

From North Carolina: "When I make starch for dark garments, I find that the starch will leave no white streaks if I color it with coffee. I think people should be told to remember this next time they starch their black linen dresses!"

KEEP THE SHEEN

From Honolulu: "Perhaps I can help others by telling them how I have learned to preserve the sheen on polished cotton.

"Never rub cake or bar soap into the fabric. Wash in warm, *not* hot, water and use a good powdered soap that contains no bleach. Rinse thoroughly in warm water. Prepare starch and use this to retain the body of the fabric. Here is the most important secret: Use unflavored gelatin, follow directions to soften it and then add about a quart of boiling water. Stir thoroughly and let it cool until it is just barely warm before dipping the garment into it. This mixture will give your garment body and luster. Iron on the wrong side first and then the right side with a medium, but *never* hot, iron."

LAUNDER TENNIS SHOES

From Pennsylvania: "Here's a hint! A lady came into the laundromat with several pairs of white tennis shoes, removed the strings, tied them in one eyelet and put the shoes in with her laundry!"

And ladies, about twenty people wrote that they put such shoes in the dryer with the other clothes!

From New York: "After washing my tennis shoes in the washing machine, I spray them with thin starch.

"This puts a thin film over the cloth and prevents the soil from clinging to the fabric. The insides are still soft and as comfortable as can be."

Overshoes and galoshes can also be washed in the washing machine along with tennis shoes. One woman wrote me that she had done this for years with excellent results.

Here is a tip for washing white shoelaces: Simply thread them through a buttonhole of a white garment before putting them in the washing machine. Tie loosely. With this method, the white shoelaces will go through detergent, bleach and a thorough rinsing and come out cleaner than after a scrubbing.

"ADD TWO BATH TOWELS—"

A tried and true method of washing shower curtains: Put the shower curtain in a washing machine. Fill this with hot water. Add *two* bath towels. Add one-third cup each of detergent and bleach. Run through entire cycle. Rinse in plain hot water to which has been added at least one cup of vinegar! Do *not* rinse vinegar out. This method won't work without the bath towels, so don't forget 'em! *Don't* spin dry. This may cause wrinkles in some types of shower curtains.

THOSE TROUBLESOME NURSES' CAPS

From New York: "The best laundering method I have found for nurses' caps is to wash and heavily starch the caps.

Do *not* squeeze them dry. This causes wrinkles to show. Just let them drip until excess starch quits running.

"Press the caps with the palm of the hand on the oven door. Ovens are made from porcelain and most refrigerators aren't. Porcelain will give an entirely different result than baked enamel surfaces such as some refrigerators have. The caps will shine like glass.

"I have also found that nylon whiteners are excellent when used in the wash or rinse water and was delighted to discover that these can be mixed with starch.

"And for mothers and bachelors who aren't nurses, did you know that this method is wonderful for hankies? Especially those lovely linen ones. These can be placed on a shower door or window for drying.

"There will be no 'shine' on a beautiful hankie as when one irons it. It will look as if it were brand new. And it only takes a few hours for hankies to dry, too."

CUT DOWN IRONING

For the housewife who uses pants-creasers: run the pants in your dryer for about ten minutes and then put them on the creasers. This removes the lint from the pants and the wrinkles from the top part of the trousers, which will then need little or no ironing.

BUTTON THEM UP

From Philadelphia: "After years of trying to untangle my husband's shirts after they came out of the spin dryer . . . I finally discovered that if I button the cuffs to the shirt front button, they won't tangle. How perfectly simple!"

"DRY OUT" THE WRINKLES

From New Hampshire: "Sometimes we get in a rush at our house and pull the clothes out of the dryer and don't have time to fold them. Then when we return to the job at hand . . . the clothes are all wrinkled.

"These wrinkles can be removed if the clothes are returned to the dryer for a matter of five or ten minutes. (The gas company loves me—but this process really remedies the 'boo-boo.')

"I have used this same method on clothes the children have thrown in a heap or that have gotten jammed together in the closet or wrinkled in any way. Five to fifteen minutes in the dryer while you are dressing will find the garment ready to wear without one stroke of an iron on the part of the busy wife and mother. You'll be surprised how much lint is removed in this process from wool and other fabrics.

"Another trick we learned when the children were small was throwing damp 'snow pants' in the dryer when they came in from play. By the time they were ready to go back outside the clothes were dry."

ALL ABOUT CLOTHESLINES . . .

From Montana: "Tell wives who are weary *never* to hang pillowcases separately on a line. Hang pillowcases in pairs . . . one over the other. When removing them from the clothesline, do *not* separate. Remove and fold together. If you are one who must iron pillowcases, iron them together, too. This cuts your hanging, folding and ironing time in half."

When hanging little girls' pants and little boys' shorts on the clothesline . . . put them over the line with both sides hanging down and just use one clothespin. When they are dry, remove the clothespin and lift off the line. The pants will already be folded and ready to be put away.

From Hawaii: "For those who want to take down three full loads of laundry from the clothesline and carry them into the house in *one* trip, clothespin bag and all:

"Simply hang a sheet between two separate lines (with three clothespins holding each hem) to form a basket! As you gather your clothes, toss them into this 'basket.' When finished, gather the bulging 'basket' tightly in one arm, remove the pins with your free hand and take the whole caboodle into the house! *All* in *one* trip!

"When sheets are not included in the wash, use large bath towels and make two or three 'baskets.' You can still manage without dropping anything on the ground! If towels aren't available you can use diapers. This is easier than using a plastic laundry basket which only takes up precious space in the laundry room."

EXTRA TOWEL BARS ADVISABLE

From Rhode Island: "I think every housewife should buy extra towel bars and place them over the bathtub . . . one above the other!

"These bars are good for nylon stockings and underwear that are too fragile to hang outside and drip so profusely. When these bars are hung above the bathtub in rows about 18 inches apart, they look very neat. They will hold all those delicate things that you do not wish to put on your clothesline."

NEW TYPE OF LAUNDRY CART COVER

From Hawaii: "For those who have trouble with their laundry cart cover slipping off or mildewing . . . I have solved the problem. I had a laundry cart cover made from flexible plastic window screening and sewed it permanently on the cart. (I suppose anyone could make one.) I had large pockets made on each side for clothespins and one pocket for small articles, such as socks, that could easily be lost while I was carrying in an armload of clothes."

SAVE TIME, SPACE

For those who use top and bottom sheets of different kinds —for example, a contour sheet and a plain top sheet—and fold them together when they put them in their closet to prevent wasting time when making the beds, here's one better!

Hang them on the line that way! Put the contour sheet on the bottom and hang the top sheet over this. Saves space on the line, too. But better yet . . . when you take them down, fold them together, thus saving two operations.

FLUFFIER SPREADS

From Galveston: "Nothing disgusted me more than to buy a pretty candlewick bedspread and have it look like a pile of knots after it was washed.

"I found that I could hang it across the line in a hard wind with the insides (this is the knotty part) together. All the little knots rub together and as they buff against each other, they fluff themselves!

"I also learned that I could put the spread on the floor and sweep it with a clean broom after it dried, and this would fluff the knots up even more."

BOIL CLOTHESPINS

From New Mexico: "I usually bring my clothespins in the house when I take the laundry off the line. But, occasionally, it will rain while the laundry is outside. The clothespins stay wet and turn dark where they touch the wet clothes. This rubs off on future washings. So I simply boil my clothespins in a weak solution of bleach and water for a few minutes, rinse thoroughly and dry well. They are like new again."

THIS IS THE WAY WE IRON OUR CLOTHES

From Michigan: "There is no law that says one must use a regulation-size ironing board. A good thick padding and cover shaped to fit the kitchen table, with some elastic sewn on the corners of the cover to hold the padding in place, makes the ironing go so much faster. The pad is easier to store than an ironing board . . . besides, it doesn't take up extra space when in use.

"When I wanted a special ironing table, I put together such an arrangement with old flannel blankets and some muslin . . . after seeing sheets being ironed in a Chinese laundry! Once this method is used, you will never use any other method.

"The next step is to catch the man-of-the-house in a reckless mood and persuade him to make an ironing table. A piece of plywood with four legs is all it takes. This table should be as wide as the widest pajama jacket or shirt and as long or longer than pajama pants . . . *plus* room to set the iron! Height should be four inches higher than the ordinary table. And this is what I had in mind when I started writing!"

FOIL DOES A BETTER JOB

From Hawaii: "The most fantastic thing I have ever discovered in all my years of housekeeping is to put heavy foil under the ironing board cover. Be sure to use a complete strip the entire length of the board. If your ironing board is very wide, then two strips will be needed to cover the padding. Then put your cover over this.

"When you iron, the heat from the iron will reflect and you will find that your ironing will go twice as fast! No wet clothes to hang in the closet! Instead of having to run the iron over the damp garment three times, once is all it takes, thus not only saving energy, but time and electricity."

SLICK TRICK

From Ohio: "When I get a new ironing board cover, I take a small piece of paraffin and iron it into the far corner of the ironing board cover. When the iron starts sticking to the clothes, I can just wipe the iron across this dab of paraffin and it glides like a whip."

DEEP FREEZE UNTIL READY!

From New York: "For years I have been putting my clothes in plastic bags after sprinkling them, and then putting them in the deep freeze. If you iron while the clothes are very cold and the iron quite hot . . . this does a beautiful job and makes ironing a breeze. I have found that clothes can be left in the deep freeze indefinitely with no harm to the fabrics whatsoever. I suggest that everyone should have a freezer, if only for this one purpose!"

SHIRT TIPS

From Kansas: "This may help those who have lots of shirts to iron: stand on the wrong side of the ironing board and use the wide end to iron them. It may seem strange at first but in time you'll find it much easier and twice as fast. First, iron the collar, then the sleeves and shoulders, as usual. Next, iron the left-front—the part with the button holes. The back of the shirt can be done in two 'moves.' It will fit perfectly on the wide end of the ironing board."

From Virginia: "For those with large families and many shirts to iron . . . don't iron the entire shirt! I see no need to iron the part that is tucked in the trousers, as it doesn't show anyway. For women who wear suits and blouses, the same applies.

"For blue jeans that youngsters wear rolled-up . . . roll the leg before ironing the pants and that saves time, too. Why should we iron the bottom part of the leg when it is rolled and tucked under?"

IRON CUT WORK FACE DOWN

From New Jersey: "I make beautiful cut-work tablecloths, but it breaks my heart to see people iron them improperly. They should know that cut work and embroidery should be ironed face down (or on the wrong side) on a *heavy* bath towel. This will allow the stitching of monograms and the stitches of cut work to stand up as beautifully as on the day the tablecloths were made. The linen, on which most of this delicate work is made, will also show every thread of its beauty."

CRAZY . . . BUT IT WORKS!

From Delaware: "Some of my coffee-drinking friends think I am a lunatic the first time they see me ironing slacks, boxer shorts, pajama pants and the like. But they invariably go home converted to my system: Pull one leg down inside of the other leg. This will look like a half-pair of pants. Iron on the wrong side. Back darts, etc., won't mark the pants because they will be together. Open to finish."

SALT AWAY THAT SMELL

Did you know . . . that if you add a teaspoon of salt to the warm water when sprinkling clothes they won't smell of mildew when the ironing is not done on time?

KEEP 'EM DAMP

For ironing large tablecloths which dry quickly, pin a Turkish towel to the end of the ironing board and double back one end to act as an envelope. Place the long item in the towel and pull it out as you iron.

DOUBLE UP

From Ohio: "To lighten the ironing load: stack handkerchiefs, napkins, tea towels and the like, one on top of the other, on your ironing board. While ironing, fold at the same time. By the time you get to the bottom of the pile, there is less ironing to do each piece. Usually, just the edges need to be ironed on the pieces left."

TRY DRIP-DRY METHOD

From Utah: "I suppose your readers hate ironing as much as I do! But do they know that ironing can be reduced to practically nothing if they will drip dry everything?

"Stop your washing machine *after* the rinse cycle and *before* the spin cycle takes place.

"I remove my garments and place them in a plastic bucket and take them to the line. I put shirts and dresses on plastic hangers. I hang everything straight. I then use spray starch as I iron and it's like magic."

SALT AWAY THE STARCH

From New York: "If starch sticks to your iron, put about two tablespoons of salt on a piece of paper and rub the iron over it. The starch will come off like magic. There is no reason to cool your iron when you use this method.

"To make your ironing easier and your iron glide faster . . . save the heavy wax paper from bread, wipe with a towel to remove crumbs and run your iron over the *inside* of the bread wrapper. Be sure to use the inside and not the outside as the coloring of the print on some wrappers will mess up the iron."

WAX YOUR PETTICOATS

From Virginia: "I have found the answer to the nylon and cotton petticoats that go limp after washing. Since they have to be ironed anyway, I place waxed paper over the petticoat and press. The wax from the paper transfers to the garment and it looks new again. This is especially good in damp weather when everything goes limp."

SPONGE SCORCH OFF

From Maine: "I wonder if people know that you can sponge a scorch off of *white* shirts with a piece of cotton which has been soaked in peroxide? I find that it comes off easily and leaves no residue, and the iron does not make another stain as you re-iron it."

From New Jersey: "If you scorch an article while ironing, just wet the goods, apply cornstarch to the spot and rub in well. Allow this to dry."

SQUIRT THAT IRON

From Pennsylvania: "Have you ever tried to put water in a steam iron (even with a measuring cup) only to spill it all over the place? I bought a baby-sized ball syringe and I find that it works beautifully when I just fill the ball and squirt the water in the iron."

KEEP IRON CLEAN

To clean steam irons: Use commercial products or pour plain vinegar in your iron. Use the same amount of vinegar as you would of water. Steam the iron for four minutes, disconnect it and let it set one hour. Empty the vinegar and rinse the iron with water. Wipe the iron over a damp cloth before using, to catch any sediment that might have come loose. You might also run the iron over a wet washcloth.

From Chicago: "I clean the outside of my iron with a damp paper towel and a small amount of toothpaste. Any brand works. Then I wipe it clean with another clean, damp paper towel. The iron must be cool to use this method. This method also shines the sides of the iron."

5.

So, Sew!

~~~~~~

NO MORE HAYSTACKS!

For those who are always losing their sewing needles, push a wad of cotton into the little hole in the spool. Stick the mending needle there. Next time a button comes off, there will be no looking for a needle in that sewing box.

Do you know that you can make a wonderful pin cushion out of a covered steel-wool ball or pad? It keeps the needles and pins very sharp.

To make machine-threading easier when sewing, cut the thread near the spool that is already on the sewing machine, tie the new spool of thread (that is to be placed on the sewing machine) to this, raise the presser-foot and just pull the thread all the way through, *including* the needle!

Do you know that blunt sewing machine needles are wonderful for ripping seams? Keep one in your pin cushion for this special purpose.

TRY THESE TRICKS

All commercial patterns call for a ⅝-inch seam. Those who sew can place a three-inch strip of adhesive tape parallel to the inside edge of the machine, ⅝ of an inch from the sewing machine needle. When sewing, let the edge of the material run along the inside edge of the adhesive tape as you stitch. This saves guesswork and measuring the seam width.

Put cellulose tape over darts on patterns for easier tracing. This will also keep the patterns from tearing.

When sewing on plastic, wax paper is wonderful. If you put wax paper over the seam, the sewing machine needle won't stick to the plastic and pucker. The wax paper tears off easily when the stitching is done.

Have problems with husband's worn shirt collar? When his collar or cuff is frayed, stop at a large department or dime store and buy (in the notions department) a new collar or a set of cuffs and simply sew on. These collars and cuffs come in sizes, too. One can even buy French cuffs. The shirts look just like new when repaired and last many, many more months.

A dressmaker told me that she often copies expensive clothes that her customers bring her, without patterns. This is her secret: Tear off a piece of foil, hold it against the garment and *press* it with your fingers! This leaves a perfect indentation where the seam is! Remove the foil and cut the indentation. This leaves a perfect pattern. When placing the pattern on the cloth, leave seam allowance around the edges. When you come to a dart . . . press where the dart is, cut (or slit) this and lay the foil down on flat material. The size of the dart will be apparent.

Whenever you have to shorten a skirt, you can use your ironing board as an aid. Stick the pins right into the padding when measuring the hem. Also . . . they need not be removed until the pressing is done. After pressing, hand-sew the hem while the dress is still on the board.

Here's a new use for those out-of-style "peasant" skirts. Rip up the sides and make two beautiful aprons! Use a harmonizing solid color material from your sewing basket for a tie and huge pocket.

One of the easiest ways to mend a hole in a garment is to place a thin sheet of paper under the hole and darn back and forth with the sewing machine. Then, when the garment is washed, the paper dissolves, leaving the garment with only the threads. This also works on bedsheets with big tears or rips.

Use iron-on-tape when lining homemade belts. This will assure sewing the material straight. Press the tape on one side of the material, along the edge. Turn the material over the belting and just press gently. Now your belts won't look homemade any more.

Socks can be mended on the sewing machine. Use masking tape to shape and hold the holes together while sewing them. Stitch right through the tape. The tape dissolves when the socks are laundered.

Here's a special use for plastic bags: Place in them any small amounts of piece goods left over from sewing. You can see through the plastic and find any certain piece of cloth that is needed right away . . . without removing all the stuff in the bag. Any pieces of cloth that you buy for future sewing, fold and place in a plastic bag, too. These lie flat and can be stored on shelves or racks. This keeps them dust-free and neat.

NET RESULT

After one year of buying, sampling, making and trying all kinds of curtain panels, I think I may save you many days of washing and ironing and some money.

I ended up with nylon net, and let me tell you why. First, it usually is less than forty cents a yard and is seventy-two inches *wide!* I bought mine over a year ago and in different colors for each room so that I could test colors, too. As net is twice the width of most materials . . . this really cuts the price of your material in half. Now just where can you get anything for twenty cents a yard? Hot air costs that much today!

Nylon net is the easist fabric to sew with that I have ever

seen. It can be purchased practically anywhere: Dime, department and variety stores. It also can be ordered through catalogues.

Net comes in a variety of shades and colors to match practically anything. The best part about it is that you can change your curtains when you get tired of them without feeling guilty about a terrific expense.

Here's the easiest way to make 'em: Measure the length you want your panels and add seven inches to each length. Buy this much material for each panel you need. Don't make 'em skimpy. If the material costs a buck a yard . . . I would advise you to skimp. But not so here.

Now, here is where you might make your mistake. Hem the top first by turning up a three-inch hem and stitching. This can be sewn single or with a casing for the curtain rod. It's all according to how good you are on the machine. The casing top makes the curtain look nicer. You can look at any curtain in your home and you will see how to double stitch it.

There is no need to turn the raw edge under before stitching. This is absolutely a waste of time, makes the curtain bulky and is a dust catcher to boot! Just stitch below the raw edge.

There is not a woman who reads this who cannot turn up a raw hem and stitch it on a machine. If you have no machine . . . use a needle and mercerized thread . . . your mistakes won't show and the fabric is light enough so that you do not have to sew for strength. No pinking shears are needed for this material. It does not ravel.

I hem all of my tops one after the other, as if I were running a production line. It's faster, neater and quicker.

If you are one who "just can't level things" and your hems are always uneven, hang one curtain on the rod first. Take your scissors and cut the hem even with the floor or baseboards, window ledge or whatever length you want them, leaving at least four inches for the bottom hem. Then remove the curtain from the window.

Lay all of your panels on the floor, one on top of the other, with the measured curtain on top of the pile and cut them all at once! This way all are bound to be the same length.

Before picking the curtains up off the floor I turn *all* of them up four inches and press with a hot iron (just lay a folded sheet on the floor under the hems) as many thicknesses as I have curtains. This leaves a guide line so that when you get ready to stitch 'em, you don't have to worry about their being all the same length. Bring all of the curtains to your machine and stitch the hems one after the other.

EASY TO KEEP CLEAN

These curtains do not have to be washed continually. I take mine down (when they get dusty) and lay them on the floor and sweep 'em with a broom! They look like new again. Sometimes they can be brushed while still on the window.

When you decide to wash these frothy curtains, *don't* use hot water. Remember, nylon is a man-made fabric that has no "pores." All that is needed is water that is *barely warm*. Hot water sets wrinkles in nylon.

Shake the curtains first to remove the loose dirt and dust. Place them in your bathtub. Cover with *cool* water and a mild detergent. Suds them gently! They need no scrubbing! The dirt will wash *off* them. There is no need to soak them.

Rinse immediately. Do *not* wring or twist. Pick up each curtain and give it a slight shake. If you have a shower curtain rod . . . throw them across that, one on top of the other. Place newspapers under the rod to catch the dripping water. Within minutes these curtains can be replaced on their rods. Therefore, no undraped windows for a day or so while you iron 'em.

Now, don't go out and buy a houseful of nylon net to make panels. Try one room first. I can make eight panels and press them (one on top of the other, all at once) in less than an hour.

BUT, REMEMBER—

Here are some drawbacks: Don't buy too dark a color when making your purchase of the net. Navy blue? No! It shows dust.

For one room, I bought pale pink. This is fine. Gray and peach are wonderful. Pale green is good too. The dust doesn't show on these. In another room I used red. Why? Because I had a red side drapery.

Watch for bargains and sales.

This is an excellent purchase for your bathroom, especially if you have a shower. I have never seen mildew on nylon net. Water won't stain it. Steam won't make it limp . . . and let me tell you about ruffles!

RUFFLE YOUR MISTAKES

Ruffles are the easiest thing you can make with net. They hide all of your mistakes, in case you aren't the best seamstress. And . . . these ruffles need not be hemmed at all! Just cut a strip of net as many inches wide as you want your ruffle. Gather it and sew it on your unhemmed curtain. That's all there is to it.

Sometimes we who have jalousie windows in bathrooms and kitchens find them hard to drape. A big ruffle can be made from this net just by gathering a long strip or two (one on top of the other) and this can be thumbtacked around the edge of the jalousie. Darling!

To wash these, just remove them from window, put them in *cool*, sudsy water in your kitchen sink and pat them under with your hands. Rinse them under your water faucet and *shake* excess water out. Tack them back on the window immediately! Isn't that fun? As cheap as these are, you can change your color scheme each month!

TRY 'EM!

Nylon net curtains are light and airy. The light shows through. They remind me of tinted whipped cream. But the best part of this is that they cost so little. Where else can we buy material for *that* price . . . that doesn't need to be ironed?

If your bedroom curtains match either your walls, carpets, or bedspread, they will make your room look larger and will not give you the feeling of having your room cluttered up.

When sewing on nylon net, buy mercerized thread that is at least two shades lighter than the material.

Go out and buy some nylon net and make some curtains today. You'll love 'em.

Index for HELOISE'S HANDY STAIN-REMOVER GUIDE

(Numbers refer to paragraph.)

6.

Out, Dratted Spots!

Here are some everyday remedies for the most "popular" stains in everyday life. And ladies, soap and detergent are *not* the same thing. Soap often sets stains. When the directions say detergents . . . they mean detergents!

1. *Butter and Oleo* On *white* linen or cotton napkins. Put in sink. Wet thoroughly and apply household scouring powder (such as you use to clean sinks) which contains a bleach. Scrub with brush. Let set until stains are removed. Rinse and wash as usual. Test for color-fastness first if fabric is colored.

2. *Candle Wax* Scrape as much as possible off of the cloth with a dull knife. Place cloth between two (white!) paper napkins (or towels) and press with a warm iron. To remove any remaining residue, sponge with a grease solvent. If safe for the fabric, boiling water may be poured through the spot.

3. *Catsup* If set by heat or age, this may be difficult to remove. On washable articles, sponge with cool water and let set for thirty minutes. Work a detergent (not soap) into the stain and rinse as usual. If stain remains after detergent treatment, use a chlorine bleach or hydrogen peroxide. A final sponging with alcohol helps to remove the detergent but be sure to test alcohol on the fabric first to see if it affects the dye.

4. *Chewing Gum* There are many methods for removing chewing gum. The best I have found is to put the garment (yes, and even a shoe) in a plastic bag and let it freeze! Then the gum will come right off with a flick of the fingernail. The plastic bag will keep frost from forming on many objects.

5. *Chili Sauce* Use the same method as for catsup, above.

6. *Chocolate* Massage glycerin into the fabric well and wash it out with plain water. If all the stain is not removed the first time, additional applications will do the trick.

7. *Cod Liver Oil* Apply a solution of equal parts of detergent and banana oil. Rub this in and then launder. If some stain remains, use hydrogen peroxide. For nonwashable materials, place a pad of soft material underneath and sponge with denatured alcohol.

8. *Coffee* Soak cloth overnight in a large pan of strong vinegar water and hang in sun while dripping wet. Better yet . . . put it directly on green grass. Then wash as usual. Or: use commercial coffee pot cleaners. Directions are on the box. Or: try commercial household bleach being very careful to follow the directions on the bottle . . . if safe for the fabrics.

9. *Dishwasher Film* Fill dishwasher with all your glasses and porcelain china. *Never* put any silver, aluminum or brass, etc., in the washer when this method is used: turns other things black and it's a mess! Put bowl in bottom of dishwasher. Pour one cup of household bleach into bowl. Run through washing cycle but do *not* dry. This is important. Fill bowl again with one cup of vinegar and let the dishwasher go through the entire cycle. This will remove all film not only from your glasses but from the dishwasher too. The sides of the washer are loaded with film! There is no use trying to get it off the dishes if it's on the washer. Remove it all . . . in one operation.

10. *Fingernail Polish* Sponge the stain with acetone or amyl acetate (buy at drugstore). Use amyl acetate on acetate, arnel, dynel, and verel, and acetone on other fabrics. Nail polish remover can also be used to remove the stains. But do not use this on the above materials without first testing the fabrics to see if it will cause damage.

11. *Formica and Micarta*   Never, never use an abrasive or strong scouring powders on these surfaces! Such treatment will ruin the finish. Pour rubbing alcohol on the surface and spread evenly with your hand. Allow this to sit for a minute and then pour bleach. Spread this over all stains. Rinse with clear water. A solution of vinegar water is wonderful, too.

12. *Fruit and Berry*   Stretch material over a large bowl and pour boiling water through stains. If stains remain, bleach with hydrogen peroxide or chlorine bleach. Camphor will remove fruit stains from table linens if it is applied *before* the cloth is wet.

13. *Grass*   Work detergent into the stain and rinse. *If* safe for the fabric, sponge stain with alcohol. For acetate, dilute alcohol with two parts water. If the stain remains, use a chlorine bleach or hydrogen peroxide. On nonwashable articles, try alcohol first *if* it is safe for the fabric.

14. *Grease*   Some grease stains can be removed by rubbing detergent into the stain. Then rinse with hot water. Grease solvents are often effective even after washing the garment. Sponge the stain thoroughly with a grease solvent and let it dry. Also (and this is the best thing I have found), a grease solvent or cleaning fluid can be mixed with talcum powder into a paste and applied on the spot and allowed to dry. Brush off and wash as usual.

15. *Ink (ball-point)*   Sponge this stain repeatedly with acetone or amyl acetate; do *not* use acetone on acetate, arnel, dynel or verel. Washing often sets some ball-point ink stains. I have had excellent results from plain rubbing alcohol when it was safe for a fabric. And did you know that cuticle remover will remove ball-point ink from leather goods? Yes—the same stuff you use for manicures.

16. *Ink (regular)*   If stains remain after the above treatment . . . treat them as rust stains. Most regular inks wash out with detergent and water.

17. *Lipstick*   Outside of commercial removers, glycerin may be applied and left to set. Wash as usual. Or: rub with lard or petroleum jelly. Wash in detergent. If any stain remains and it is safe for the fabric, rubbing alcohol or hydrogen peroxide may be used. Wash as usual.

18. *Match Streaks*   On some items these can be removed by cutting a lemon in half and rubbing the sulphur marks. Be sure that the item can tolerate lemon juice!

19. Mercurochrome and Merthiolate Soak overnight in a solution made of four tablespoons of ammonia to each quart of warm water. Or: sponge with alcohol diluted with two parts water . . . if safe for the fabric. On nonwashable articles, if alcohol is safe for the dye . . . sponge with alcohol for as long as any of the stain is being removed. For acetate, dilute alcohol with two parts water. If stain remains, place cotton pad, saturated with alcohol, on stain and keep pad wet until stain is removed. Be sure alcohol is safe for the fabric.

20. Mildew Government booklets say to treat this while fresh, wash thoroughly and dry in sun. If stain remains, treat with chlorine bleach, sodium perborate bleach or hydrogen peroxide. Our readers say . . . soak in naturally soured milk overnight. Rinse and expose to sun until dry. Another method is to rub salt on stain with lemon juice and place in sun. Ammonia suds usually remove mildew from a rubber gasket.

21. Mud Let mud dry. Brush out most of it and soak in *cold* water, then launder. If stain remains, use denatured alcohol.

22. Mustard On washables, apply glycerin (can be bought at any drugstore, and cheap). Work into the stain and then wash thoroughly with detergent solution. *Never* use soap. Rinse as usual. Or: rub detergent into the stain after dampening with water. This may be allowed to soak overnight if the stain is bad. After rinsing, if the stain remains—use sodium perborate treatment if it is safe for the fabric. If safe . . . alcohol may be used. Dilute with two parts water for use on acetates.

23. Perspiration If possible, wash thoroughly with warm water and detergent. Apply diluted ammonia to fresh stains and rinse with water. Apply white vinegar to old stains and rinse with water. Remove any yellow discoloration with sodium perborate, but test fabric first.

24. Shoe Polish On fabrics that are applicative . . . try rubbing alcohol. This works most times. Test fabric first to see if the alcohol is safe for the material. Or: on some fabrics cleaning solvents may be used. Especially on paste wax. If stain remains, use glycerin or mineral oil. Work into the fabric and then use cleaning fluid. Remember, if safe for the fabric, rubbing alcohol removes much residue.

25. Sink Stains Household cleanser (scouring powder type) which contains bleach may be made into a paste and rubbed *on* the sink. Leave this overnight. Rinse as usual. This often takes away stains that have been there for a long time.

26. Tea Same applies to coffee. Commercial coffee pot cleansers will remove most of these stains. Or borax solution will often do the job, too. Use one teaspoon of borax to one cup of water. Soak. Rinse in boiling water. If stain is fresh, pour boiling water from a kettle or pan from a height of two feet through the stain. If any stain remains, use hydrogen peroxide and rinse well ... *if* safe for the material. Test a spot first.

27. Tobacco Use rubbing alcohol! Apply with a wash cloth or a piece of cotton. Rub stain. If alcohol is not safe for the fabric, use directions for grass stains.

28. Toilet Rings These are not rust stains, but rust removers will eliminate them! Liquid rust removers are faster than paste types. (Buy at a drug, dime or department store.) Just lower the water line in your toilet and apply. "Rings" from a build-up of mineral deposits may be removed with sandpaper ... after the water line has been lowered. Usually plain sandpaper of a fine grade is all that is needed. If the ring is "years" old ... it may require using wet sandpaper (available at hardware stores).

29. Yellowing of Drip-Dries Household bleach sometimes turns drip-dries and crease-resistant clothes yellow and dingy looking. Never use bleach on "treated" cottons. When "treated cottons" become yellow, the discoloration can be removed by soaking the garment in a hot solution of any commercial color remover.

WRITE FOR BOOKLETS

For additional hints, send fifteen cents to the Superintendent of Documents, U.S. Government Printing Office, Washington 25, D. C., and request the booklet entitled "Removing Stains from Fabrics, Home Methods."

For those who have mildew problems: write to the Superintendent of Documents, U.S. Government Printing Office, Washington 25, D.C., and ask for a booklet called "Home and Garden No. 68 on How to Prevent Mildew." Send ten cents.

QUICK TRICKS

Equal parts of turpentine and ammonia will remove paint from clothing even if the paint has hardened.

Sometimes, BATHTUB STAINS just do not take to household cleaning. Especially the stains caused by the rusty pipes which some apartments have. Fill the tub with water (so the bottom of the tub is completely covered), add lots of bleach and let this stand overnight. The next morning you will have a sparkling clean tub. If your rubber mats are badly stained . . . throw them in, too.

A waitress told me how to get GRAPHITE (from lead pencils) out of nylon and dacron uniforms: she applied the type of hand soap that mechanics use, took a soft brush and scrubbed, and it worked.

If a third of a cup of vinegar is poured in your baby bottle sterilizer and left to soak overnight, it will remove the MINERAL AND RUST DEPOSITS.

You can remove the YELLOW from treated white cotton shirts by using color removers that come in boxes. Follow directions on the box, using only enough for one shirt at a time. One package will whiten four or five shirts, depending on the size. Works on dacron and cotton too.

After washing SOILED TENNIS SHOES in the washing machine, apply white shoe polish diluted first with one-half water and when they are dry any stains are completely covered and they look like new!

A woman asked how to remove UNDERARM STAINS on a nylon slip. The stains were caused by a dress that faded. The only thing I've found that will remove these stains is alcohol! Just plain rubbing alcohol. Pour some on a wash cloth and rub the spot.

A woman told me to warn readers that some of these deodorant bath soaps, when used on clothing to remove underarm stain and odors, will remove the color from the material, too! She used a bar of this type soap to remove a spot on her daughter's pink dress and was left with a faded spot.

A woman wrote: "I have just ruined a good black crêpe dress and don't know what to do. I dropped a little BLEACH right down the front and it bleached it white. Can you help me?" My answer to her was: If you can't afford professional help, try using black shoe dye on the spots. It usually works beautifully. I have tried it twice and when the dress was cleaned it did not come out.

Another woman wrote: "I have a faille coat that is practically new but the left sleeve is shiny from the handle of my purse. The tailor said he could not remove the SHINE." I answered: If you will dip a terry wash cloth in warm vinegar (straight) and wring it out well . . . then rub the spot hard . . . all shine should leave. This will also work on navy and black gabardine and black crêpe dresses. Do *not* get the fabric wet. It should need no pressing at all.

Baking soda in water left to soak in plastic cups will remove COFFEE AND TEA STAINS.

For RUST in a stainless steel sink: rub with lighter fluid until the rust disappears, then go over it with scouring powder and the sink will look like new. As an added *caution:* lighter fluid is flammable, so do not use near flame or fire, and keep it out of reach of children.

To clean the STAINED COPPER BOTTOMS OF POTS AND PANS:

pour a little vinegar on the bottom of the pan, then sprinkle some table salt over it. No rubbing is necessary. Wash and rinse as usual. This can also be made into a paste. If you want to make your own paste, mix one-third of each . . . salt, vinegar and flour. Let set a day or so. However, I do not make the paste personally. It is just one more "jar" to sit under my sink and the salt and vinegar are always near by, so why not just pour it on?

An inexpensive SCRATCH remover for natural wood cabinets and woodwork is mineral oil. This blends into the wood and assumes its shade as well as polishing the wood at the same time.

There are many uses for pecans and walnuts and peanuts. The meats from these nuts are wonderful for removing scratches from all kinds of furniture. Just remove the meat from its shell and break the nut in two. With the broken side of the nut meat . . . just rub the scratch gently. The oil from the nut meat will eliminate any discoloration and your furniture will look like new.

To remove white WATER MARKS from table tops, etc., apply mayonnaise and rub it in. Let stand and wipe clean with a soft cloth in an hour or so.

To remove PAPER that has stuck to the top of an end table, pour furniture oil on the paper and let it soak for a while. Overnight is best. After the oil soaks into the paper thoroughly, rub with a soft cloth and this should remove the paper and not harm the furniture finish at all.

A favored way of removing CRAYON MARKS from woodwork is to use kerosene on a soft cloth such as a wash rag. Most landlords use this method. Remember, kerosene is flammable —be careful! Paste wax will remove crayon marks from furniture if the wax is applied on a cloth and then wiped off. If the crayon hasn't all disappeared on the first try, repeat. This will also work on enamel and painted woodwork. Another way to remove crayon marks from woodwork is a plain piece of dry cotton material. Just rub the marks gently. This applies also to plastic table tops, linoleum and glass.

MILDEW MADNESS

For MILDEW in closets, on shelves and walls . . . dip a cloth in plain, straight household vinegar and rub all the mildew from the wood. Let dry thoroughly. Always clean all the mildew from the walls before painting. About mildew and mold in closets: many people keep a light bulb turned on all the time to check the mildew problem. A young woman sent us this tip: "I took mildew off my nice red leather chair by just waxing it with plain paste wax. Paste wax has more body than liquid waxes. After applying the wax, I rubbed the spotted leather thoroughly with a cloth and the mildew came off with the excess wax."

IF YOU WEAR YOUR SPAGHETTI . . .

A reader of my column sent this: "To remove SPAGHETTI SAUCE STAINS, I soak the garment in cold water for at least thirty minutes. Then I rub one of the liquid-cleaning agents into the spot. I wash colored clothes the usual way although the water might be a little warmer than usual. Whites are washed in hot, hot water. Usually the spot leaves immediately, but if a trace remains, use diluted bleach with an eye dropper."

FLOOR PLAN

For removing DARK MARKS on floors: these marks come from rubber heels and from rubber tips of some types of kitchen furniture which have some black carbon in them at the time they are manufactured. The cheaper the heels, the worse the marks. Pure rubber heels leave no marks! These marks can usually be removed by mopping with a solution of trisodium phosphate and water or something similar. If there are any really obstinate marks, then lighter fluid will undo the worst. This evaporates so fast that it will not do any harm. However, if the lighter fluid is spilled on the floor and not immediately wiped off . . . it may leave a mark or spot all its own. Lighter fluid should *never* be left where children can get to it. It is dangerous. Read the directions on the label.

MAHOGANY MAGIC

SCRATCHED MAHOGANY woodwork can be repaired by painting the scratches with iodine. After applying iodine, go over the entire surface with furniture polish and this will eliminate any noticeable defects. For EBONY furniture, use black liquid shoe polish or black eyebrow pencil. Wipe this with a furniture polish cloth.

AH! THERE'S THE RUB

If anyone has dropped ALCOHOL on asphalt tile and caused white spots, rubbing a little baby oil on the spots will remove them.

For BURNS on rugs where the scorch cannot be removed entirely: take a thread pulled from your carpet to any good stationery store. Buy a crayon that exactly matches, and rub in on the rug. It will help blot the spot. It worked for me although the spot was not entirely through to the back of the rug. This method also will cover any stain on clothing that can't be removed any other way.

THE APPLICATION'S THE THING

Did you know baking soda or corn meal will remove GREASE spots from carpeting? Simply pour a generous amount over the spots and brush lightly through the pile of the rug. Leave it overnight and vacuum off the next day.

For removing PET STAINS on carpets: treat immediately as they can affect fibers and dyes. Most cannot be removed satisfactorily.

Blot up as much of the moisture as possible with towels or tissues. Sponge repeatedly with clear water. Blot again. Apply vinegar and water solution; blot dry. When rug is thoroughly dry, sponge with detergent and water solution and blot dry again. Place dry white towel over stain and weight down with a book until completely dry so the remaining moisture can be absorbed through the "wicks" of the rug into the towel. If the towel becomes damp, replace with a clean, dry towel.

Another method recommended by a professional rug cleaner: Use club soda, straight from the bottle and not diluted. Use "towel procedure" above for necessary drying to prevent further spots or rings.

COLOR YOUR SHOES WITH CRAYONS

Here's a useful tip from a neighbor: "I have tried about everything there is to polish multicolored shoes which are so fashionable today. Let me give you my answer! Colored crayons!

"I bought a box and now I can always match each color exactly no matter what shade the shoes are. Just take a crayon and mark on the shoe wherever it is skinned. Buff with soft cloth. All SCUFFS are gone immediately. Skinned places are hidden beautifully.

"I even use the brown crayons on my son's shoes, especially where the toes are scuffed. Red crayon will suffice for daughter's little red shoes if you ever happen to be out of that red polish.

"But the beauty of it all is that multicolored shoes can be

matched perfectly and you don't have to buy nine different colors of polish. There is only one drawback to this: Hide the crayons where the kids can't find them. If you don't . . . they won't be there when you need them."

DYE YOUR OWN SHEETS

Here's a tip for wives who love colored sheets but don't have the budget for them: When stores have their sales on linens . . . buy the white sheets and pillow cases, which are much cheaper. Then buy two boxes of all-purpose dye and follow the directions on the package for automatic washers. The sheets come out beautifully. Two packages of dye are enough for two big sheets and a set of pillow slips (and maybe a blouse or slip). Old sheets can be dyed this way and they seem almost new.

When white nylon or dacron turns YELLOW, try a tint. After wearing white nighties and slips for some time, it perks you up to have a color. I find the best colors to use are turquoise and peach. Different tones of pink can be mixed with the peach color.

7.

Pestered by Pests?

~~~~~~

HOUSEHOLD PESTS BESIDES IN-LAWS

Bothered by beasties you've been unable to control? Don't be self-conscious about it—sooner or later all households are invaded by these little monsters. Let's consider ways to get rid of them.

"BUILD A BETTER MOUSETRAP"

If mice are in your kitchen, look for a hole near your drain-pipe under the sink. Use a piece of steel wool to stop up any such holes. Use a knife to stuff the steel wool tightly in place. A mouse will not eat through steel wool. If you still have mice, look for another hole near the hot water heater base where the pipe goes through the floor.

From New York: "We live in an apartment building that is overrun with mice. For the last six months I have put moth balls everywhere. And no more mice in our apartment! They just do not like the odor."

THE POWDER TREATMENT

"Little armies of ants come in my kitchen door and cluster around near the entrance," a woman wrote to me. "Is there any home remedy for this? I am afraid of poisons because there are too many kids and pets about the place."

This is what I told her: "If you are afraid of commercial products, try this: pour talcum powder around your door or window, or wherever ants are coming in. They say ants don't dare cross it! If you can possibly find the ant hill . . . any poison may be poured directly into the hole with safety.

Some people use boiling water and scald 'em. Others use a commercial product."

LOOK WHERE THE IVY TWINES

This was a query on mosquitoes: "We live in an apartment and have our troubles—mosquitoes! I have looked everywhere and cannot find their breeding place. As this is winter and there are no swimming holes or fishing places near here and we seem to be the only family in the building that fights the buzzards, I would appreciate any help you can give me."

My reply: "I believe that I have the answer for you! As you live in an apartment and seem to be the only ones bothered by these 'buzzards,' I can bet that you have ivy planted in water all over your apartment! Ivy is a favorite breeding place for these little creatures. I am going to tell you how to run a test to see if I am correct.

"Pour the water out of one vase into a fruit jar, filling it about three-fourths full. Be sure not to fill the jar to the top. Screw a cap on the jar.

"Set the jar aside for a few weeks and *see* what develops! I bet you will find some creatures within a few days that look like microscopic tadpoles. Within another few days they will get bigger and soon you will see mosquitoes in the air pocket atop the water in the jar. If this is so . . . then you are the one who must change the water each week to prevent their breeding. The mosquitoes won't do this for you!

"There are two ways to change the water. The hard way is to remove the ivy, empty the vase and fill it with new water. The easy way is to set the vase in your sink, turn the tap water on and let the water run into the vase in a medium stream. This will cause motion and agitation and the larvae will go right down the drain! This only takes about five minutes.

"Now . . . be careful not to put the vase back on a beautiful table and make a ring. I suggest that you change the water at night before retiring and put the vase on your drainboard overnight to drain.

"Another thing that I do is wash the ivy leaves themselves. I do this by turning the spray hose on full force and spraying each leaf. Garden shops taught me this. If you are really an avid ivy-grower . . . did you know that the leaves can be rubbed with cream or milk? Just dip a cloth in either and rub each leaf. They will shine like glass."

THE USDA WAY

From a woman in Virginia: "I have read with interest about beetles and weevils in kitchen cabinets. I've had the same experience.

"Beetles were all over my cabinets and even in the cabinets below the food. After trying many things, I contacted the County Agent of the U.S. Department of Agriculture, and the suggestions I got finally did the trick.

"Empty your cabinets completely and throw away *everything* not canned. This takes courage, for it is a seemingly extravagant and wasteful procedure. However, I found larvae within tightly sealed cartons, even though the contents were not infested.

"Remove all canned contents and wash the cans with a strong solution and a brush. Rinse well and allow to dry. Wash the entire cabinet with a similar solution, let it air and dry. Spray cabinets with a good beetle-bomb and leave them closed for a while. All of these procedures should take place the same day, because if you don't do this all at once the beetles will move to untreated territory during lapses.

"As you replace your stock of uncanned foods, put them into glass jars or tin or plastic containers with airtight lids. Never keep a plastic bag or paper box in your cabinet.

"I have never had bug trouble since I did the above purging! Occasionally, I have found a beetle in a glass jar of starchy food, and have thrown the food away immediately. I have also learned not to have such a large quantity of foodstuff on my shelves that it must sit for a long time. Once beetles come into your cabinet, they travel *fast* from one paper container to another. Glass jars put an end to this. Just any jar with a screw lid will do."

This woman is exactly right when she gives you this information. I would like to add a few explanations:

I have cleaned many cabinets where friends couldn't get rid of weevils. They cleaned just as she said but . . . they wouldn't throw away that half-empty box of ice cream cones, etc. At one home I was told that the box of cones was new. We left the cones in the food cabinet and six weeks later the woman called and said she was "taken over" again. Sure 'nuf, I picked up her box of ice cream cones and guess what I found? We lifted up the top cones and the bottom of the box was all *air* and bugs! The little devils! They had eaten all her cones.

I have advocated that people use fruit jars for containers after they bring foodstuffs home from the store. It doesn't take long to pour something into a jar. The reason: *if* you bring home something from the store that just happens to have bugs and put it in a jar with a screw lid . . . the bugs can't jump from one jar to another and infest other things. Another good thing about the fruit jars (besides being cheap and free) is that if something does get bugs in it . . . you can *see* that the devils have taken over again and discard the infested merchandise.

But the best thing I like about fruit jars—and they come in many sizes—is that you can see how much flour, meal, etc., you have in your cabinet. Ever get ready to cook corn pone and not have enough meal? *Wow!* As for the directions on the packages, tear off the recipe and stick it inside of the jar.

You can also take an ink marker and write what each jar contains on *glass*. Or didn't you know this? When you get ready to put something else in the jar . . . just use a soap-filled pad and scour the original writing off.

HAVE YOURSELF A ROACH HUNT

From Pennsylvania: "After fighting roaches with preparations and never getting rid of them, I decided to go looking for 'em!

"I found roach eggs on draperies, on rope in the cupboard and on crocheted pieces I had tucked away in a cabinet.

"I found scads of eggs around the motor of the refrigerator, and this was the main breeding place. I could always find baby roaches (dead) in the tray underneath the motor. This tray catches the water from the defrosting. Taking a flashlight, I looked above the tray and I was shocked at the eggs hanging from the lining around the motor! I took my vacuum cleaner and sucked all of these off the lining. I now do so every once in a while, and I have gotten rid of roaches.

"Roaches, I have discovered, lay eggs on anything they can cling to. I even found eggs hanging on the rough underpart of furniture. I took drawers out of the cupboard and found eggs way back in the dark places. I even found them on the rough iron under the sink.

"After reading this you will think I really had roaches and, believe me, I did! But until I found the eggs and destroyed them, I could never get rid of them.

"For anyone having roaches in the family car, I wouldn't be afraid to bet that the eggs are under the seats where the stuffing and springs are."

Now, if you want to find some more: look under your dining room chairs where the corners are glued for reinforcement! These little devils love glue! Your coffee table and end tables probably have the same thing. Remember, too, that underneath all the drawers in your dresser and closet, the same thing is happening. It's dark. And they love that, too.

If you suck them up with your vacuum cleaner, be *sure* to empty your cleaner after using it. It will be dark and warm in there and they will multiply fast. Now, if you want to put out bug-juice, the time to do it is when you are cleaning these spots. Paint it on while those drawers are open.

Remember that your hot-water heater in the closet—or any place that is warm and dark or has any dampness (such as your dishwasher or sink)—is a good breeding place.

Also, under your dishwasher, under your stove (just look underneath the burners where all the grease has dropped), your wall oven (after you have removed the broiler), under your bathroom sink and the water closet back of the toilet! Your washing machine is not only warm and dark but damp, too—and that dryer! The tops of these two gadgets usually pull open (or the back does). Get your husband to open it up and look at the cobwebs that will be filled with eggs.

Also, just look back of your book shelves! Remove all those books, dust 'em with your vacuum attachment and apply the bugkiller.

Remember, darkness, heat and moisture are potential breeding places for roaches. Look any place where you might find these.

One house I went to had all these places cleaned. Yet it still had roaches, and guess where I found loads of eggs? Not in the kitchen cabinet but in the curtain rods and headings of all the draperies!

Draperies (especially if they are the heavy draw-type) are seldom cleaned. The pleats at the top are usually filled with eggs! The little devils also get into the curtain rods! Look inside a curtain rod and see for yourself!

Gals, don't waste your time putting bug-juice out unless you put it on the right places. There's no other way to really get rid of these pests.

8.

Personally Yours

~~~~~~

"A PENNY SAVED . . ."

Who doesn't want to know another way to save? For those of you who buy hand creams, thick lotions and cosmetics in bottles, I have just learned how to get the last bit out of each bottle.

When you can no longer shake the bottle (or squeeze it . . . and some bottles just won't squeeze the last bit out) hold it upside down under the hot water faucet and let the water run over it for a few minutes. Be sure the lid or top is on. Once the heat from the water softens the contents, the goo will run down to the lid in the bottle.

Now open the lid! You will be amazed at the amount that will come out! I pour this into an old cosmetic jar while it is thinned from the heat. Then I use it later.

And did you know that you could mix lots of things together when you get down to the last dab? I mix hand lotions, liquid facial creams, cleansing creams, etc. It's great to wipe some on your face just before that quick bath.

QUICK FACIAL

Another thing, all wives don't have time to cream their faces. We are just too busy. While running your bath water, if you will slap some kind of cream on your face and then take a hot washcloth (wrung out) and hold it over your face for a few minutes . . . you will surely notice a difference. The heat and dampness from the hot water in the cloth gives you a real cleaning! I am not one who has time for facials but this is the quickest way I have found to get relaxation and a good cleaning!

For soap pieces: I tie these in a square piece of white nylon, then I hang the bag with the soap pieces in it on the bathtub water faucet.

When I take my bath, I let the water run through the bag.

SURE, YOU HAVE TIME FOR A MANICURE!

I suggest that women break up all their backbreaking jobs around the house into three or four sessions and work in a little beauty treatment, too! Then everything will get done without any strain.

This works wonderfully for a busy housewife—for instance, one who has no time for manicures. Keep the manicure set handy and break up the manicure into different sessions. Eventually, you will have a manicure without sitting down thirty minutes for this project.

Between the jobs of answering the telephone and doing the laundry and dishes, take the old polish off. This only takes a few seconds. Later, file one hand or both according to the

amount of free time you have. Then, later, use that cuticle remover and get the hangnails. Even later, you can either polish one hand with two coats of polish or both hands with one coat of polish. Eventually, you will have a complete manicure.

The same idea goes for other housecleaning jobs. Nothing is half-so-bad if done in spurts when you're in the mood.

TRIM YOUR LIPSTICK, GIRLS

If you use a razor blade to slice off the end of your lipstick tube diagonally, it will give you a very sharp outline when applied. It seems to fill out those minute wrinkles and cracks around your lips. Put the discarded lipstick ends in a small jar and use them with your lipstick brush.

SET YOUR HAIR WITH BEER

Stale beer is a good solution for setting the hair as it gives the hair "body." Just dampen the hair and roll. The hair will not retain the beer odor when dry. Many beauty salons use this method. Another good trick: when pinning up your hair, a quick way to dampen it is to fill a spray bottle with some water and spray the hair wherever needed.

PUT JEWELRY ON DISPLAY

An unused picture frame, a piece of corrugated cardboard and a bit of black velvet material can make an attractive "display case" for pins and brooches which frequently overflow jewelry boxes.

Remove the glass from the frame. Insert the corrugated cardboard (cut to the exact size of the glass), and cover it with black velvet material. Now you can hang your "display case" on the bedroom wall, within handy reach of your dressing table or chest of drawers. Stick your pins and brooches artistically into the velvet-covered cardboard—and your jewelry boxes will be less cluttered, your bedroom unusually decorated.

These are really conversation pieces. Also, when other gals come in they always want to know where you bought such and such a piece of jewelry. If you are tired of it . . . that's the time to trade it off! The prettiest pair of earrings I have came from one of these "display" boxes. This is the thriftiest way I know of to get new jewelry!

You can clean costume jewelry by putting it in a little bowl and pouring rubbing alcohol over it. Let this sit a few minutes and all tarnish will come off. After wiping, the jewelry will look like new.

SWEET TALK

If you want to be real fancy when having company, put a few dabs of cologne on a piece of cotton and wipe the phone.

This leaves it shiny and free from dust, and it retains a delightful fragrance. The alcohol in the perfume also acts as an antiseptic.

MAKE YOUR OWN RAINCAPS

As plastic head covers aren't the prettiest things for rainwear, try this: cut a triangle from a plastic bag and insert it in a head scarf. This is waterproof. By folding the scarf over diaper fashion it doesn't show. When the rain stops, simply remove the plastic.

DETERGENT HANDS?

Many ladies complain that detergents hurt their hands. This could be caused by using too much detergent and keeping one's hands in it too long. Try stacking dishes before washing them and using only half as much powdered detergent in a dishpan of hot water. You'll have lovelier hands because you are cutting the amount of detergent in half and you'll probably still get the same results with the dishes as before, but look how much you'll save on soap bills!

One woman told me that while she was arranging the contents of her deep freeze, her hands were smarting with cold. She suddenly thought of her asbestos glove, and found that it was equally as effective as a protection from the stinging cold of the deep freeze as it was from the heat of a fire!

SAVE THOSE PUFFS

Don't throw away dirty powder puffs and spend good money for new ones. Just wash them with your clothes, put them in the dryer, and they will come out looking like new. This way you will have a fresh puff continually and your complexion will look better as you will not rub the oil and dirt back into your skin.

Never remove the cellophane that covers the top of a box of face powder. Instead, soften the cellophane with a hot towel and prick a dozen or more holes in it with a sewing needle. Then you will be able to shake enough powder for daily use into the cover of the box. This way, the puff doesn't touch the rest of the powder and it never spills.

SHAVE YOUR SWEATERS

Knots that appear on sweaters can easily be removed by taking a piece of *fine* sandpaper and gently rubbing over the knots. They will "go" and the sweater will look like new. Knots can be removed with a razor, too. *Carefully* shave 'em off! Lots of people shave sweaters!

I have learned to turn a sweater wrong-side-out and button it up before ever washing it. Thus, the outside doesn't rub against other materials, which help cause these knots.

Here is a simple idea for girls and women who wear sweaters and washable jersey blouses. It will save lots of time spent in pressing. Wash sweaters and washable jersey blouses in cold water with a cold water soap. When rinsing, squeeze, never wring.

Roll sweater loosely in bath towel to remove excess moisture. Remove from towel and lay on kitchen table. Take your roll-

ing pin and roll over the sweater (just as if you were making a pie crust), making sure the sweater is stretched out smooth. Over the sleeves, where you want a nice crease . . . roll several times. Then lay the sweater on a towel to dry. Your sweater will look lovely and your friends will think you have spent hours steam pressing.

This works on bulky sweaters and knit dresses, too.

KEEPING WHITE GLOVES WHITE

Most of us wear white gloves, and a friend would like to pass on a good cleaning method.

Mix liquid detergent in the wash basin with warm water (add some bleach if necessary) and then put on the gloves. Wash as if you were washing your hands. Use a nail brush to get the tell-tale spots off the fingertips! Remove the gloves, then rinse by holding each glove under the faucet and filling it with water. Hold the top of the glove and squeeze while it's still full of water. This will completely remove all the soap.

This method will be just enough to get them clean but not enough to cause the discoloration you might get from using a pure bar of soap between the hands and washing the gloves.

QUICK TRICKS

Masking tape is a good de-linter and is a very fast method for removing lint on anything. Just press it on the garment, whether it is a hat, coat or husband's best navy blue suit. (It'll also pick up dandruff.)

There are plastic bottles on the market with a little brush attached to the top. These are recommended for cleaning pots and pans, woodwork, dishes, and so forth. I have found an even better use for them. I fill the plastic bottle with shampoo and use the brush when washing my hair. The brush is a marvelous scalp massager and the container being plastic eliminates the possibility of broken glass if you should drop it.

Small pants-creasers (size 6-9) can be used in women's tapered capri pants. They are exactly the right size, and this gives 'em a good crease and saves on the ironing.

Iron the veils on hats between wax paper. The slight bit of wax will transfer to the fabric and restore crispness. This also seems to keep veils on hats from drooping in damp weather.

Many women lose their diamond rings by removing them and putting them in different places around the house. The best place to put your watch and rings when removing them is on your powder puff! You will never forget to put them back on and will always know where they are.

Knot your nylon hose in pairs when taking them off and

leave them this way while washing and drying them. This works well and saves hunting for mates.

Nothing makes me as angry as snagging a good pair of nylons with a clothespin. I cut off the fingertips of some old cotton gloves and slipped them over the tips of the clothespins. The result was wonderful! These are snagless clothespins. I now use them for all my fragile garments. It also prevents rust marks and soil from the pins themselves.

When hanging nylons or leotards outdoors to dry, slip a teaspoon into each toe. This prevents the hose from wrapping around the clothesline and getting snagged.

I cut my old slips off about ten inches below the waist and wear them for camisoles under my blouses when wearing slacks, etc. In winter they are warm. They fit much better than anything I can buy.

Having trouble drying your crinoline petticoats? Just put them over an open umbrella! Great!

Here's a cookie for you: To make wooden coat hangers hold low-cut dresses and "spaghetti" straps . . . just wrap some rubber bands around each end, where the shoulders go. This will keep the straps from falling off the hanger.

For those who have suede jackets and can't afford a cleaning bill every week . . . I clean mine beautifully with a little suéde brush (the kind I clean my shoes with) and go over it with a wash cloth that has been dipped in vinegar and wrung out well. Sure saves on cleaning bills.

9.

Pointers on Practically Everything

~~~~~~

FOREVER BLUE JEANS

A woman asked me what to do to lengthen boys' blue jeans. "My boys grow fast," she said. "I buy the extra long legs and hem them up but when I let them down, they have a horrible white line and the boys say: 'Mother, it shows and looks awful.' Also, what's the best way to iron them? I have twelve pairs a week."

My reply to her was that when I let down my son's jeans I use a dark blue crayon and mark over the white line. Then

press. The heat from the iron makes this just about permanent! The blue crayon will cover the white line. I have found this does not wash out easily and lasts quite a long time. If it does wash out it's very easy to take that crayon and make another mark.

And why on earth iron jeans?

Anyone can buy a pair of pants-stretchers. They cost only about 50 cents a pair. Buy six pairs. If you can't afford them all at once . . . buy two pairs each week or month. They are worth it . . . in the long run they will pay for themselves.

You will save on the electricity your iron is using when you press 'em. And think of not looking at that stack of blue jeans each week! When using pants-stretchers, just take the pants off the line, fold 'em and put 'em away.

But, honey chile, most of all . . . you will be relieved of the drudgery each week. Think of the hours you save!

Here's how to hang jeans:

After they come out of the washer and have been spin-dried, stack them all up (along with anything else you don't want to iron, including pajamas and husband's shorts). Then take a pan of hot water and put it under your clothesline. Dip the garments into the water and hang them up. Then put the pants-stretcher in the jeans. The weight of the water will pull wrinkles out of garments and save ironing many things.

So take life easy. Learn the easy way to do things. If you are one who starches blue jeans . . . the pants-stretchers will also take care of that problem easily. They can be used with starch, too.

"DOT" YOUR EYES

Bad eyesight is an asset sometimes. It's one way to help others . . . so I found out!

For years, I got angry every time I set the thermostat on my oven. *Why* don't manufacturers make the numbers larger so we can see 'em? I cannot understand this. Don't they realize that the older we get . . . the harder it is to see that old court-house clock? The radio dials? And the thermostats on every-thing?

I am in my forties and find that I must hold a newspaper a little closer; I must squint to find the hole in the needle; and I gripe when I am in a hurry to cook biscuits and I can't find the 450° mark on the oven.

That is, I did until I resorted to fingernail polish . . . every woman's household stand-by! A red "dot" on appliance dials will save you squints and spells of temper.

I have enjoyed this vision-aid for months now. All I do when I get ready to bake bread is "hit the red mark," which I put on the 450° marker on the oven. It's terrific! Saves time when it's most important.

After a week of using this, I discovered other things. We all have our favorite radio stations . . . put a red dot on them, too! And on your favorite TV channel. This only takes a few seconds and is worth so much time later. Just think of the times you turn a dial. Try it. If you don't like it, it can be removed at no cost.

Daily, weekly, monthly and yearly . . . just how much time do you actually spend *looking* for that exact number?

SOUPING UP THE SOAP PAD

I wonder how many of you go into your kitchen and pick up that soap-filled pad that you used the day before and start to clean a pan . . . only to find the pad rusted? This makes housekeepers mad. I can't blame you . . . but worse than that, it's wasteful. For over six months now, I have been using a new method to prevent this waste. The pads will last a week or two if this method is used.

We all have old sugar bowls which we never use. Where are yours? On a top shelf somewhere . . . where no one ever sees 'em? What are you saving these beautiful sugar bowls for? You never use them at Sunday dinners or for company. Why? Because they are on the top shelf! Learn to live, gals. Get that beautiful sugar bowl out and put it on your drainboard where you can see it three times a day and use it three times a day.

Now . . . put your soap-filled pad in that sugar bowl. Let the hot water faucet run till the water is steaming hot. Fill the sugar bowl with this hot water until it completely covers the pad. Put the cover on and forget about it for a day.

Know what you will find the next day? A goopy cleaning agent that is the most wonderful thing you ever saw! It can be used for days and days. But the best part about it is that your soap pad will be soft and pliable and will last for days . . . and not rust!

With this soft pad . . . you can clean better and you can *rinse* it out each time you use it. Example: When we clean a pan in which scrambled eggs or mashed potatoes have been cooked, the pad always gets dirty. We hate to rinse a pad that is filled with soap for which we have paid good money. Not so here! Rinse the pad under the faucet and replace it in that beautiful suds-cleaner that you will have in your bowl.

If you don't have a sugar bowl . . . use a peanut butter jar.

I did for months until my eye caught that sugar bowl on the top shelf.

If your water line gets below the soap pad, just add more water. Be sure to keep the pad *under* the water. No rust will come. I have used pads for as long as two weeks this way.

USE THE BEST WHILE YOU CAN!

What I am trying to tell you sweet housewives is that there is no one more important in your home than *you!* So don't save your good things for "tomorrow"—use them now. Life is so short—enjoy every day of it.

Get your good silver out and put it in your kitchen drawer and use it every day. Use your good dishes at least once a week, if not daily. There is no one who will ever come into your home who is more important and loved any more than your own family. They are the greatest!

If you could only read some of the letters that come to me saying such things as:

"Heloise, I never knew how much I loved my husband until he was gone. I ate off old dishes, saved my good silver for company (and none was as good as he) and covered my beautiful satin comforter (the one he gave me) when I should have used it so that the beautiful satin would show and he could see it! If I had it to do over . . . Tell the young ones to enjoy their families and use their good things."

So go get that pretty sugar bowl out and so what if you put a soap pad in it? At least you are enjoying it daily!

GET YOURSELF A PAPER ROUTE!

The easiest way I know of to wash dishes without getting your hands wet is to use paper plates! This is a real timesaver.

Expensive paper items are available but are quite unnecessary. Some paper plates are half the price of others. True, you can't use them for cutting steaks, and they aren't very good when you have waffles with lots of syrup, but for sandwiches and salads they are grand.

When buying them, another way to save is to get smaller sizes. The little salad size is perfect for sandwiches, with a small salad or pork and beans. These are cheaper than the large size and take less room in your cupboards.

I am of the opinion that most mothers with small children don't eat a good lunch because along about noon their homes are getting clean and they don't want to dirty the kitchen and do dishes all over again! If paper plates are used, there is no need to have your kitchen dirtied again. Very small paper cups are cheap, too. Not the big ones (compare prices)— probably all the kiddies will drink is a small glass of milk, anyway.

Using paper plates and paper cups leaves you with only forks to wash. And that can be simplified: If you place dirty silver in a glass of water it will not only soak the food off but most times will prevent tarnishing from things like potato salad. Don't bother to wash silver at noon. Leave the glass in your sink, where it doesn't show, or on your drainboard.

On the subject of paper plates and cups, I know you are thinking: "Why spend money needlessly for extra items that I can do without?" Have you ever thought how much it costs you to wash dishes for one meal?

Figure this way . . . You must have hot water. How much does it cost to start the thermostat on your heater? How much does the soap cost? How many dishes do you break? How much to launder that dish cloth? How long does it take? Time is of the utmost importance to mothers, and energy even more so.

Add these figures up and include the time you spend doing the dishes. Keep the figures for two weeks. Then decide. You can clean up a "paper lunch" in two minutes. It takes about thirty minutes to wash dishes, dry them and put them away.

Caution: I did not say you should buy the best, heaviest and biggest paper plates. Buy the cheapest. They are also grand for that late snack of a piece of cake or pie. And no dirty kitchen in the morning!

PEN-POINTER

I received a note from Nevada: "I've got a good one for you and it works. The subject is ball-point pens. Everyone accumulates them and when you get down to writing with the ones you've stashed away . . . you find they won't write!

"Light a match and heat the ball-point tip slightly. Usually the ink will start running again. If you open up the pen and see that all the ink is dry, then, of course, this won't work. But eight out of ten times all it takes is a lighted match."

Please note: Be sure the pen filler is metal! This method will *not* work on plastic ones. The plastic melted on the one I tried. For plastic fillers—just bring a small amount of water to boil, place the fillers in the water, make sure they are covered, and turn the heat off. As soon as the water is cool enough, remove, wipe dry and replace the fillers in the pen holders.

QUICK TRICKS

From Navy wife: "If your readers have trouble transferring a pie crust from its rolled-out state to the pie pan and it ends in patches and full of tears . . . here is a hint which I have learned from a Navy cook aboard my husband's submarine. He uses a length of broom handle and rolls the crust out with it, using only one hand. Then, beginning at the edge of the crust, he rolls it up on the broom handle . . . then unrolls it into the pie plate."

A man from Manhattan sent this: "I can't explain how this works, but I put tea in a coffee can and pour boiling water over it, place the lid on the can and steep for about five minutes. I've used all kinds of tea pots to make tasty, clear tea and this method beats every one."

Wipe a little glycerin on windows and bathroom mirrors and buff with a soft cloth to keep them from steaming up.

You can't slice a straight piece of bread or bologna? Keep your eye on the main portion and *not* on the piece being cut. You'll be amazed at the result.

Instead of whittling a candle at the base to make it fit in the candle holder . . . I hold the end in a cup of very hot water for a few minutes to soften the wax . . . then gently and firmly press it into the holder.

From Brooklyn: "I tried starching my throw rugs to keep them flat and they still wrinkled, curled and were a mess. I finally took a paint brush, laid the small rugs on the dining room table that had been covered with paper, and painted them with two coats of clear shellac, letting one coat dry before applying the other. This has stiffened the fabric on the backs of the rugs and allows them to lie straight. One word of caution: be sure they are dry before placing back on floor."

From Michigan: "When shag rugs become limp from too many washings, I lay them (right side down) on a flat surface after washing them. Then I brush strong liquid starch on the backing over the entire rug. Just let this dry, and the rug is as good as new."

From Chicago: "I have found that when I remove my window screens for cleaning or painting, if I number them with a ball-point pen on the edge and number the window where they fit, I have no trouble getting the right screen in the correct opening immediately. Saves me lots of temper."

From New Jersey: "I always set the timer on my stove to

remember things. This really helps on Sunday mornings when we're hurrying to get to church—and I have a fifteen-minute warning signal."

If two drinking glasses are stuck together, one inside the other: fill the inner glass with *cold* water and set the other glass in hot water and they will come apart easily. The cold water causes the inner glass to shrink slightly and the hot water will expand the other glass just enough so that they will come apart with no breakage.

PETTICOATS IN THE PANTRY

From New Hampshire: "The finest labor-saver I've found is a square of nylon net—the kind petticoats are made of. It's the best scrub cloth—just scratchy enough, but not rough enough to hurt anything. (Even the net which evening dresses are made of is wonderful.)

"It's good for cleaning counters, stove tops, ovens, painted surfaces and just about everything. It's particularly good for use as a dish cloth or for taking sticky foods (such as eggs, mashed potatoes, and rice) off of dishes and pots before they go into the washer. It will even remove a light burn on frying pans.

"This nylon cloth rinses out clean and is very durable and inexpensive. A yard of net is seventy-two inches wide and sells for about forty cents a yard at dime and department stores. One yard can be cut into eight eighteen-inch squares, and it comes in all colors.

"It's a fine conversation piece, too. Almost everybody who comes into my kitchen looks and wonders, even if they are too polite to ask!

"This cloth doesn't sour or smell. Even when cleaning a pan that has had mashed potatoes in it . . . all you do is run the cloth under the faucet to rinse. The pan becomes clean immediately."

PIPE THIS

A hint came from Dallas: "We have one of those nice wall dispensers for paper towels, wax paper and foil. It was wonderfully efficient except for one thing. Everything tore off easily and evenly when a fresh roll was being used, but near the end . . . exasperation!

"The rolls just wouldn't tear off right. Our solution was to drop a ten-inch length of lead pipe inside each roll before putting it in the dispenser, and it works like a charm."

WHEN YOU NEED A FIRM HAND

Just what do you do today when you must use a food grinder and there is no old-fashioned dough board to fasten it to?

Get an old inner tube, cut a big hunk out of it and keep this in your kitchen drawer. When you use the grinder, place this on the edge of your table or kitchen stool and clamp the grinder on over the piece of tube. The grinder won't slip.

This same piece of tube (if you cut it big enough) is wonderful for getting a grip on stuck jar lids.

NOBODY BUT YOU WILL KNOW

For those who have wallpaper in their homes: When patching a spot, never cut the patch with scissors, but tear it in a round shape(or long and narrow, depending on how bad the spot is you are going to cover), and then paste the paper on. By tearing the paper, it makes a feather-type patch and is not so noticeable as when cut in a straight line.

Wallpaper does fade. When using a patch of the new paper to repair the spot, put some of it in a window in the sun for a few days or so until the new paper fades to the degree of the mellowed wall.

A dime store art gum eraser will remove most marks on wallpaper—especially around the light switches, or where little hands hit the door as they pass by.

HOW ABOUT A MAT-MOP?

A woman wrote to me and asked what were the two best things in my home. My answer was . . . an ice pick and my Hello-ease mat! The Hello-ease mat is made from an old bath mat.

Double the mat over so both sides will have chenille and sew or staple the edges together. Throw this on your kitchen floor (great for bathrooms, too) and when your kid spills water or, more common, Daddy spills an ice tray, take your foot and move the Hello-ease mat across the spills!

Saves back aches, time, getting the mop (which is usually dry and must be wet to sop up spills) and tempers.

The mat should never be over one foot square. Throw it into your laundry each week.

MEMOS FROM THE MISCELLANEOUS FILE

For those who have small children and see spoonfuls of sugar spilled each meal . . . or worse, two and three spoonfuls wasted in the bottom of a bowl of cereal . . . if you put sugar in a big kitchen salt shaker, it's easier for the kids to use.

When airing clothing outside on the clothesline, use two coat hangers instead of one, placed together in opposite directions. They will not blow from the line.

From Oregon: "When I bake a cake and want it to stay fresh a long time, I cut the cake in half and cut the first slices from the center of the cake. I then push the two halves together and the cake doesn't get dry on the cut sides. This will result in fresher cake for small families."

When lunch boxes smell bad, wash them with plain soda water, rinse, and allow them to dry in the sun. Also, use wax paper sacks in lunch-box packing. Then are wonderful to put that little slice of pickle in. Or an olive. Or a sliced tomato. Makes the lunch so attractive and enjoyable . . . cheap, too!

When using part of an onion for cooking, you can put the unused portion in a tightly covered jar in the refrigerator. It keeps for a long time and your refrigerator will not smell.

From Canada: "Those little recipe card holders make wonderful boxes for addresses and telephone numbers."

Contour sheets will go on the mattress much easier if you fix diagonally opposite corners first. Try it and see.

From Hawaii: "When lots of ice is needed for a party or picnic, fill a plastic bucket with water and place it in your deep freeze overnight. This ice *lasts!* But do not use a metal bucket as this might split. Plastic gives just enough."

From Louisiana: "I am surprised that people don't know how to clear the air in the bathroom by striking matches. Floral deodorizers are fine in summer, but in winter, with heat on, they just don't mix for us."

From Chicago: "Steel wool may be bought without the soap for much less. Pull off what you need and rub on a bar of soap or dip in detergent to make your own soap pad. The best part about it is . . . what isn't used up can be rinsed in hot water. Then shake out all the water you can and let dry. You soon learn not to pull off too much steel wool and can just throw away the used bit after cleaning."

From Maine: "About the trickiest thing I know how to do is fasten two metal curtain rods on the inside of the closet door so that shoes can be hung on them."

STEAM IRON WHILE YOU SLEEP

If the clothes crush in your suitcases while you're traveling, remove the clothes and place on coat hangers when you get to the hotel or tourist court. Turn on the hot shower (pull the curtain shut) and close the bathroom door until the bathroom is full of steam. Then go into the bathroom, open the shower curtains (turn off the shower) and hang up the clothes on the shower rod. Go out quickly and close the door. In the morning your clothes will have nary a wrinkle.

This is best done just before retiring, as the bathroom will be full of steam for an hour or so, and the door should be kept closed.

Another way is to hang the clothes on the rod, fill the tub with hot water and leave overnight, but this will not remove the wrinkles as well as the steam shower method.

FOILING THE DUST

"I have a way of protecting my good books from dust and would like to share it," a man from New York wrote me.

"Cut tinfoil (the new sandwich size is perfect) about three inches wider than the thickness of the book. Then open the back of the book, and cover the pages of the book with it. Fold it inside the two bookcovers. Close the overlapping edges neatly as if it were a package. When I read the book, I fold the foil neatly and use it as a bookmark."

PINCH-HITTERS

From Florida: "So often when we move we don't have the right size curtains for windows. I use candy-striped kitchen towels and they pinch-hit beautifully. Just stitch a hem along one end and put them on a curtain rod until you can do better. Mine looked so pretty that they are in permanent use now!

"These window curtains do not have to be striped or even all in one color. If the window is wide, put up four different colored towels on one curtain rod. They may be tied back or left hanging straight."

BRIEFLY . . .

Knitted ties that husband has discarded make wonderful covers for wooden coat hangers.

Sometimes it is difficult to screw a wood screw into wood. I first coat the threads of the screw with soap and then it's easy to set.

I find that if I take my measuring tape and press it between two sheets of wax paper, it gets new life.

ANSWER TO THE PLASTIC PROBLEM

From Oregon: "My plastic chair bottoms were very attractive with rounded seats and piping . . . until a child split three of them wide open. I tried several times in vain to cover them and finally it occurred to me that my trouble was that I was using cold plastic. This is almost impossible to work with.

"I then placed my heating pad on a work table, turned it on high heat, and cut the plastic after it was warmed. I cut the material one inch larger than the surface to be covered. I placed this material on the heating pad (right side down), placed the chair bottom on top of this and thumb-tacked one side to hold it in place.

"Smoothing every wrinkle and tacking the three sides with regular upholstery tacks, I then removed the thumb tacks from the remaining side and finished with upholstery tacks, too. It worked wonders for me."

KEEP 'EM SPARKLING!

Here's a trick for those who wash fruit jars and put them away, only to find them cloudy and molded inside when ready to use. After washing them, let them dry completely. Put a large piece of newspaper inside the jar and put the top on the jar. The newspaper will absorb any moisture. When ready for use again, your jar will be bright and shiny without any mildew, moisture, or mold.

THE LOWLY SHOE BAG

Shoe bags are wonderful things. They can be put in many places. In the hall closet is one good place. In the winter they hold mittens, extra mufflers and knit caps. The children can find their things easily. No more lost accessories.

A shoe bag in the pantry or a cleaning closet holds all those spray cans of wax, whisk brooms, clean dust cloths, vacuum attachments, extension cords, etc. Everything is handy.

And did you know that the shoe bag can be made at home easily from bargain remnants of material? This doesn't take good sewing because who sees shoe bags? Beginners can make 'em.

TELL YOUR HUSBAND!

From New Mexico: "Here's a way to save money on razor blades," a man writes. "Use a jar big enough for your razor to drop into. Fill it with just enough mineral oil for the head of the razor to be covered. Keep the razor here after rinsing and using it. Use a jar with a lid. My result? Fifteen shaves from one razor blade . . . and I have a tough beard."

SWEET SMELL OF . . .

From New York: "My mother has a grand way of making the house smell good. She just puts a few drops of oil of cinnamon in her vacuum cleaner bag and as she cleans the carpets, the air smells as if she is baking apple pies. It lasts for a long time after she has finished vacuuming." You can use any odor you prefer—oil of lemon, for instance, is great.

PUT THE TV TRAY TO WORK

From Nevada: "TV trays are wonderful, even though they cost a couple of dollars.

"The trays can be removed from the stand and used for bed trays . . . which most of us can't afford. Place two pillows across the lap and lay the tray on top of the pillows.

"I also use them with the stand when hanging laundry. Here's the easiest way I have found. Remove two trays from their racks. Place these on top of one another . . . next to your washing machine. Leave one tray and stand near your clothesline. As each tray is filled with some wet clothes, carry this to your clothesline and place it on top of the standing TV tray. When these clothes are hung, take the empty tray back to the washing machine for a refill! Oh, the energy and stooping I have saved by using this! Now my back doesn't ache on washday."

MEMOS FROM THE MISCELLANEOUS FILE

Beware of putting ammonia in your mop water! I have found that this solution has broken down many bindings on asphalt tile. It won't be noticed until you remove all those coats and coats of wax . . . then your floor will be like sandpaper. Messy, messy, messy!

For those who paper their own walls, rolling the paper on the ceiling with a paint roller is "the thing." This makes the paper smooth, leaves no wrinkles, and it doesn't tear as easily.

Shopping should be an adventure once in a while. Go to a new section of the city and pick a different store. See new things, put zest back into your life.

Save that foil insulated bag that ice cream comes in. It's great to put rolls in for warming in the oven.

From California: "I empty the dust bag from my vacuum cleaner *before* I vacuum. Then if any dirt is scattered in the process, it can be vacuumed up while I am cleaning."

To protect the arms of an upholstered chair or sofa, use small terrycloth fingertip towels with fringe on each end . . . in harmonizing or contrasting colors. They cling to the chairs, can be laundered frequently, and require no ironing. These little towels even cover up worn spots on old chairs and sofa arms. They can be used on chair backs, too . . . especially if husband has an oily head.

From New York: "I keep a big cork in my kitchen drawer and stick thumb tacks, pins, etc., into the cork. You'll be surprised how many times you'll use them in the kitchen. The pins and tacks are much easier to remove from a round cork than to lift off a flat surface."

If you are short of shelf space in kitchen cabinets, put a small shelf about three inches wide across the back of one lower shelf to hold spices, flavorings, etc. Condiments will be easier to find and this saves lots of space.

You can make do with wire coat hangers when drying drip-dries if you remove the cardboard covers that come on the lower part, punch a hole in the center of the cardboard and slip the hook of the hanger through this hole. The piece of cardboard will form a "shoulder" for the hanger and leave no "line" when a garment is hung to drip-dry. The cardboard can be secured with staples or tape. Sometimes the weight of the clothes will hold the cardboard on if you don't want to bother with staples.

WAX WRECKS PAINT JOB

From Georgia: "I suggest that people ask a good honest painter what he thinks about putting wax on woodwork and window sills. In several different apartments we had the problem of peeling paint. It was always traceable to waxings done by previous tenants. No matter how well a painter washes a waxed surface before repainting, apparently it all can't be gotten off. We have solved the problem by not waxing but painting the window sills and other vulnerable spots each year."

FOR STUBBORN SHAKERS

From North Carolina: "I discovered an easy way to open glass, silver or aluminum salt-shakers when the lids had corroded and fused to the shaker. After soaking in hot vinegar, with some salt added in very stubborn cases, my lids came right off and the corrosive material washed off easily."

SAVE YOURSELF—AND MONEY!

From Virginia: "Why do women pick up a heavy bottle when a small one will do? Pour your liquid detergent in a small bottle. Punch a tiny hole in the top of it with an old, heated ice pick. The small bottle looks much nicer sitting on your drainboard. Squirt when needed. But the best part of it all is when I pour the detergent in the bottle, I add half water! The detergent lasts longer this way and cuts my soap bill in half. Try it. Not so hard on the hands, either."

GET LAZY SUSAN TO HELP

From Pennsylvania: "What used to be my torture chamber is now my pride and joy . . . that underneath-the-sink closet which is usually a mess. I took a Lazy Susan (which I never would use anyway) and covered it with wax paper and placed my supplies of soaps, detergents, etc., on it. Now, with a spin of the finger I can get to the product I need immediately."

TWO JOBS IN ONE

From New York: "I just moved (which is usually a job) but this time instead of packing all my dishes in papers . . . I wrapped them in face cloths, bath towels, cup towels, wash cloths and anything that was in my linen closet. Presto—I unpacked clean dishes which could go right on the shelves without washing and the linens back into the closet. This also eliminated many cartons of waste paper and dirty hands."

"A STITCH IN TIME . . ."

From New Jersey: "I have just found a wonderful way to 'mend' my husband's pants' pockets. I do it *before* he gets a hole in 'em! I just add a piece of iron-on tape . . . all the way around the bottom. This reinforces the pocket and should last the life of the pants."

QUICK TRICKS

Grease the "threads" on glue and nail polish bottles and they won't stick.

Wind yarn around a few moth balls if it will be some time before you use it.

If you place a small piece of cotton in the fingers of rubber gloves, it will help prevent holes from long, pointed fingernails.

How to mend rubber gloves? The only thing we know of is moleskin foot plaster. This is not a brand name but a type of plaster that is used for corns and bunions! Buy it at drug counters.

From Nevada: "I have found that if I wax my shelves before lining them with shelf paper the paper will not stick to them. Also, if something is spilled . . . it's easier to wipe up."

Don't discard those handy gadgets that spray things. Remove 'em. Save 'em. They will fit on nearly any bottle top . . . direct! Many things can be put into bottles and the "gadget" used. Examples: starch, water, ammonia and even liquid hand creams and bleach! Save them and use the spray tops to apply all kinds of stuff.

ROTATE CLOTHING

This hint is a must for anyone who wants to save on clothing bills: rotate clothing as it comes from the cleaners and laundry!

Husbands who wear uniforms will invariably grab the first one in the closet. Husbands who wear white shirts to work will grab the top one on the pile! I know it is habit to pile shirts on top of shirts and hang suits and uniforms where they are most convenient. But—put clean shirts on the bottom of the pile, and hang clean clothes at the back of the closet.

Regular cleaning and laundering prolong the life of clothing. White shirts get yellow and deteriorate, and if you doubt this just go look at the shirt on the bottom of your husband's stack! If it's yellow, he won't wear it without laundering again.

KEEPING COFFEE HOT

Anyone have a vacuum bottle seldom used? Get it out of the cupboard today. Wash it. Next time you have a cup of coffee left over, pour it in this. Cap. The coffee will keep hot all day long. Never bitter, and no waste.

TRY A PAPER GLOVE

Keep a small paper bag handy when mixing dough, just in case the phone or doorbell rings. If it does . . . slip your hand into the sack and open the door or lift the receiver without getting dough on it.

PUT BOTTLES TO USE

From Pennsylvania: "When you buy food seasonings or condiments in glass bottles that have perforated plastic tops . . . save the empty bottles. Wash and let dry thoroughly. Fill with flour and use this to sprinkle meats or make gravy! Real handy. Such bottles are good for the bathroom when filled with water softeners or bath salts. Even cleaning powders for the tub and basin. These bottles can be spray-painted or decorated with sequins, etc."

THAT HANDY FOIL AGAIN

Here's an idea for those who are too frugal to buy plastic coat hangers for their drip-dries. Cover wire coat hangers with foil! Cut the foil in one-inch strips and wrap round and round. These strips can just be folded on the three sides of the coat hanger and pinched together.

MAKE A MEMO

From Connecticut: "After I wallpaper a room, I write with a pencil on a wall (behind a picture) the amount of wallpaper and border it took to do the job. Also the date. Next time the room needs papering . . . I know exactly how much to purchase."

THE WAX TREATMENT

From Michigan: "Summer and winter. Two seasons entirely different. Stuck bureau drawers come with both. After fifteen years I've found a pretty good solution.

"I use any old wax, such as a candle or the paraffin from the top of a glass of jelly, and rub on the sides or runners of the drawers wherever they stick. Another solution: wax bread-wrappers. These seem to be heavily coated with wax. Lay the bread wrapper on the runner of the side of the sticky drawer and open and close the drawer until the wax is gone from the paper."

PRY OFF A SNACK

Save the covers from cottage cheese and dip packages. Wash and dry. When you have collected about a dozen, buy three or four pounds of ground beef on sale. Lay a cover on the drainboard and put one-half cup of meat on the deep side (top) of the cover. Press with your hand and stack one on top of the other for freezing. When you want a late snack, just pry one or more off the stack and there you are! The lids can be used many times.

FREEZE LEFTOVERS

From Brooklyn: "Ice trays are good for something else besides ice. It finally dawned on me that I was spending money on containers in which to put cooked food and leftovers for deep freeze storage.

"Now I line an ice tray with wax paper (two thicknesses) and pour my leftover food in them. Freeze. When hard as a rock, just remove from the ice tray and replace in your deep freeze by folding the wax paper over and using rubber bands.

"Money, time, and costly containers saved. Most of all . . . frozen food may be quickly thawed this way, as it is thinner. Also, chunks of these long, narrow blocks of food may be broken off and only pieces reheated for lunch. What a saving to break off a half-block of leftover spaghetti when only that much is needed."

CATCH THE SPATTERS

A colander can be inverted over a skillet when frying anything where grease is popping—bacon, chicken, etc. Heat escapes but spatters are caught on the colander. Saves cleaning the stove.

PACKAGE YOUR GARBAGE!

From Illinois: "Milk containers, especially the two-quart size, are the answer to the daily garbage problem. They can be used in two ways. Open the top completely and push your potato peelings, tomato culls and excess lettuce into the box, then fold top and discard. Or leave the original top closed; using a paring knife, slit the box on the side. This is wonderful for times when we have lots of garbage. The side-slit method holds about twice as much. When the box has been slit on the side (in circular fashion or V-shape), just push the home-manufactured top down into the box and it will hold."

IN BRIEF

For the people who boil eggs in an aluminum pan and don't like the pan to turn dark, just add a dash of vinegar to the water.

From Denver: "When making ice in empty milk cartons that contain lots of wax, rinse the inside of cartons with hot water first to melt and remove most of the excess wax. Then fill with cold water. If the carton still contains wax after freezing (and you will know after testing a few) run the carton under hot water again before using, remove the top, and the block of ice will fall out. I rinse ice again before using, as I never know on which day the dairy is generous with wax. I do find plastic cartons foolproof."

Here's an idea from Canada: Put a paper pie plate in the bottom of your waste basket and it will keep the basket clean and keep it from rusting.

From Ohio: "I have just learned that when peeling apples for apple pies, you shouldn't throw the peeling away. I put all my peelings in a dark aluminum pot and boil them in water and it makes the aluminum bright again. Cream of tartar will do the same thing but it is more expensive. For this method, use one tablespoon of tartar to a pot of water and boil thirty minutes. Saves lots of scrubbing."

It's a chore to get a pastry brush clean. One woman makes

her own disposable kind with a clothespin and a small piece of paper toweling. Just clip the paper in your spring-type clothespin. Brush your pastry or baste your meat and toss away the paper towel.

If you take a soiled sheet from the laundry hamper when you are about to settle down to a sewing session and place it under your sewing table, you can take it to the yard and shake it after sewing. This is a great time-saver as you do not have to clean all the little threads and mess up from the floor after finishing a garment.

From Detroit: "Lining drawers? I have the answer. I buy plastic place mats. These can often be bought on sale in odd designs. It makes no difference if the designs don't match as one never has two drawers open at the same time anyway. These make the best drawer liners I know of. They are stiff and flat and one swipe with a damp sponge and the drawer is clean! They are very easy to cut with scissors and may be cut into any shape."

Another suggestion from New York: "Line your drawers with pretty paper and then take one of those plastic cleaning bags and cover the paper with it. Allow a few inches on each side to turn under. Place this in your drawer and use thumb tacks to hold the paper down. The paper will always stay clean and if one should happen to get some water in the drawer . . . it can be wiped up easily with a sponge without spotting the paper."

For a good inexpensive dust cloth, use a soft absorbent old cloth sprinkled lightly with water and then sprinkled lightly with furniture polish. Roll this up and let stand a few minutes. Removes finger marks as well as dust.

If you buy a little one- or two-cup dripolator (the regular coffee pot type) and use it for bacon drippings, it will save lots of trouble. The "drip" part in the pot catches the little odd pieces of bacon and all of the clean fat goes to the bottom of the pot. When you are ready to use the fat . . . just pour from the drip spout! Looks much nicer on your stove than a can, too!

Plastic bags may be used to store out-of-season shoes. Also to store extra ice cubes in the deep freeze, for damp wash cloths for sticky hands and faces in the car, keeping sandwiches fresh, and to store carrot sticks and tomato wedges for picnics.

PREVENT MARKS

To prevent unsightly scratches on walls, caused by furniture being pushed against walls, you can buy "rubber bumpers" with little nails attached for inserting in the backs of furniture. Look for them at your dime store or hardware store in the nails and bolts department. Some people call them rubber stoppers.

I found that if one of these "bumpers" was put on each corner at the bottom of the frame on heavy pictures, a picture would not make a mark on the wall and . . . the picture would stay straight.

Of course, you can make your own bumpers with erasers and small nails.

For those who have metal bottoms on the legs of their kitchen chairs (flat and about the size of a quarter) . . . remove the little piece of cork that comes inside the cap from a soft drink bottle and glue it onto the bottom of the metal strip. This eliminates those nasty marks on your floors and adds a bit of a cushion so that the chairs do not leave such deep dents.

And another thing, those little flat corks are wonderful to glue on the bottom of vases and ash trays to keep the furniture from being scratched.

WEATHER NOTES

From New Jersey: "My husband keeps an old windshield wiper blade beneath the front seat of his car and in the mornings when the dew is heavy, he uses this to clear the glass . . . back, sides and front, before hitting the heavy morning traffic."

If snow shovelers will wax their shovels with paste wax they will find the job of shoveling snow much easier.

ANCHOR YOUR TOWELS

From New York: "Here is my suggestion for keeping your bathroom towels anchored! I happen to have towel racks that are removable without unscrewing . . . so it was very simple: I just stitched a casing (a hem) on the ends of several towels and slipped the towel bar through the casing and hung the towel bar in place. This thought hit me while searching for pins."

MAKE YOUR OWN FUNNEL

By cutting a plastic bleach jug in half, the top can be used as a funnel with a handle. The bottom can be used to clean paint brushes in or to store miscellaneous items. The funnel is handy for pouring paint into other containers, too.

TRY THESE

Line the inside of a double-faced powder puff with silver polish . . . then all you have to do when washing dishes and you come across a piece of silver that needs polishing is dampen the puff and wipe!

From Honolulu: "An empty tuna fish can, from which the top and bottom have been removed carefully, makes a wonderful gadget for poaching eggs. Place can-ring in skillet with water and drop egg in center."

To prevent food from sticking to a frying pan: Wash the pan, put it on a low burner just long enough to warm it . . . then wipe the inside with wax paper. If the pan is really in bad shape, this process may have to be repeated each time the pan is used for a while until it returns to its original condition. Electric frying pans may be treated the same way.

If you rinse a pan in cold water before pouring milk in it to heat (such as when making cocoa), the milk will not stick to the pan. This saves a mess when it comes to washing it.

BED-MAKING SHORTCUT

From Boston: "I have found that when making the bed, if I pull the top sheet and the blanket as close to the head of the bed as possible, then fold the sheet back over the blanket a few inches and use three diaper pins and pin all this together . . . I eliminate many hours of bed-making over the months. Also, it ends fumbling with the sheet and blankets at night!

"I later discovered that I could put the bedspread *under* this same edge which was folded back, and pin that, too, with the same pin. This all goes under the pillow, doesn't show at all and does away with blanket dust.

"I now just air the bed and pull the whole shebang up and smooth it out . . . with one pull! This is a great idea for children's beds when they are learning to make them."

THAT FOIL AGAIN!

To keep ice cubes from sticking to the bottom of the tray after some have been removed, put aluminum foil in the bottom of the tray. Cubes come out easily.

HAVE SOAP, WILL TRAVEL

Suitcases: When putting them away, place a bar of toilet soap in each to keep them smelling nice. It is not wasteful as the soap can be used next year. Also, sometimes we forget to pack soap and this is a good reminder.

KEEP CHILD'S BROOM HANDY

From West Virginia: "I discovered a miracle when I dropped some dried beans all over the floor. (Usually it's rice or peas or cereal.) My little girl's broom was on the floor. I picked it up to use it and discovered that it would fit between the washer and the wall, underneath the dryer, the dishwasher . . . just about anywhere. I then discovered that it was wonderful to sweep spilled ashes into the dust pan. Not at all clumsy like the big broom. Every mother should have one."

Another good use for a child's play broom: It is marvelous

for cleaning the bathtub! Sprinkle scouring powder in the tub, wet broom and scrub, then rinse. Saves back aches! These little brooms are cheap. Buy one at your dime store toy department.

From Illinois: "The grandest thing I have is my child's little toy carpet sweeper. I sweep up crumbs from the carpet under the dining table. This saves getting the big one out. This is my 'silent butler.'"

"WASH" USED FAT

From South Carolina: "Most housewives have grease left over from deep-frying 'stuff.' And the grease is black and unattractive.

"Well, I can 'wash' any fat or grease (except oil) by simply boiling the grease with water for a few minutes—then letting it cool off. When cold grease is mixed with water, place this on the heating element of your stove and let melt; simmer for a few minutes, then turn off and let cool. The black particles will sink to the bottom of the water and the grease can be used again. I also find that every taste and smell (such as fish, etc.) is gone, too."

BOTTLE LEFTOVER SOAP

Put slivers of leftover soap in a squeeze bottle and add some warm water. Leave the bottle by the basin where the children wash their hands. It lasts for ages! When the suds get thin . . . put in more soap chips. If it gets too thick, just add more warm water from the tap. This is a good way to save scraps of soap that we ordinarily throw away.

KEEP MOP CLEAN

From California: "I have found that the easiest way to keep a mop clean is by soaking it overnight in a detergent solution. Solutions of suds that have been used for soaking clothes and even dishwater will do the trick! I add some pine solution to this for disinfecting and deodorizing purposes. Several rinsings with cold water will remove the dust and grime. Drying it in direct sunlight is the final step to a sanitary mop."

ON DEFROSTING DAY—

From Maine: "My washing machine stands next to our refrigerator and I keep all the food in it when defrosting.

"I put a piece of foil or heavy brown paper in the washing machine (mine is a top loader), fill this with the ice from the trays, place the food in and close the lid while defrosting is taking place.

"After replacing the food in the refrigerator, I remove the paper and pour hot water over the ice and let it spin down the drain."

SAVE ON POCKET WEAR

From New York: "If anyone's husband is like mine and carries lots of pens, papers, etc., in his shirt pocket while working . . . apply iron-on mending tape to the underside of the shirts at the pocket corners and the pockets won't rip or tear off so easily."

INSTANT WORK TABLE

From Arizona: "When I need extra counter space for baking, etc. . . . I pull out a cabinet drawer and put a pastry board or tray across the open drawer. When through cutting the French bread (or whatever), I just wipe the board over the sink and close the drawer. I have also found that when cooking near the stove, the drawer nearest the stove is the best place for this setup."

KEEP IT CENTRAL

From Virginia: "My pet hate is trying to find an electrical outlet for the various appliances when cleaning through the house. I have to stoop behind this chair, move that table, detour around that piece of furniture, etc.

"Well, I solved that little problem. I use a long extension cord and plug it in a centrally located socket. I can now vacuum the entire house without changing the cord from plug to plug, hook up the waxer, the iron (while I watch TV), or even the hairdryer while I sit at the dining room table to polish the silver. Pretty cute, huh?"

LET THE FLOOR DO IT

From Michigan: "Instead of ironing your best linen and lace tablecloth for special occasions . . . save the effort. Besides, it never looks nice when ironed. Just dampen it thoroughly and wring it out lightly. Then spread a large sheet out on top of a rug.

"Stretch and pull as you pin the cloth with ordinary straight pins onto the sheet . . . being sure to stretch as you work along the edges. The pins go into the rug in order to hold the whole thing in place. Then put another sheet on top of the cloth just in case some child or animal walks over it.

"When the tablecloth is dry, unpin and lay the cloth on the table where it is ready for use. There will be no wrinkles or puckers in the cloth, and the whole job takes only about fifteen minutes.

"I have done huge tablecloths this way . . . the kind you don't dare send to the laundry, and ordinarily would take hours of ironing."

REPORT ON DISHWASHERS

For those of you who have electric dishwashers: See how much time the machine takes to go through the complete cycle. Then test and see how much time it takes for the dishes alone to dry.

I have tested three different brands of dishwashers and this is what I found:

You can save on electricity by turning the dial to "off" after they finish washing . . . just let them dry themselves! And why not? The washing water is so hot that it has already sterilized them and you aren't going to use them anyway until the next meal!

DO YOU HAVE A "BUTTON BANK"?

From California: "I take an empty peanut butter jar (or mayonnaise jar) and have a fairly wide slit cut in the top. This is our 'button bank.' When I am cleaning and find buttons on the floor that the children have pulled off, or find any in the washing machine, I drop them in our 'button bank.' It saves a lot of time when I do the mending. The very button that you are looking for usually will be in the 'button bank.' I keep the 'bank' on a shelf that is handy for everyone; even the kids enjoy putting buttons into it."

GOOD TO THE LAST DROP

Never throw away a box of detergent without first rinsing out the box with warm water. You will be surprised how many suds are left in the box. Enough to do another sinkful of dishes!

SAVE MONEY

From Massachusetts: "Use those plastic milk cartons to freeze foods in! I find these stack beautifully and cost nothing! I have also found that if you do not have enough to fill a complete carton, the carton can be cut with a butcher knife to the correct size. I leave a little piece on the side which I just fold over and use rubber bands to tie the top."

More uses for those plastic bottles that today's detergents, etc., come in: You can use a knife or a pair of scissors and cut vases or pencil holders for that cluttered desk. Vary the sizes and make little cups for holding hair clips, pins and the like.

With shaped plastic bottles, cut off the top part *and* the bottom part. Fit these together to make a cup with a lid. Leave the screw-cap on to pick it up with. These are grand for your scouring pads. Also for junior's marbles!

And everyone knows how glass jars and bottles on the shelf of the refrigerator door have a knack for falling out and breaking. This problem can be solved by putting all dressings, sauces and syrups, etc., in empty plastic bottles and marking the containers with a freezer-marking pencil! Should they fall . . . no more breakage. The black markings are very easily removed with household cleanser.

10.

P.S.—Some Closing Thoughts

~~~~~~

Now that you have read this book, I hope you will want to accept the facts and tell yourself that you are just one of the multitude. I am!

I want to thank each of you who has taken time to write to me to share your problems, thoughts, heartaches (those made me grow and gave me better understanding, made us close friends), and especially your wonderful household hints which have been shared in this book.

I only wish that I could come into your home and sit at your kitchen table each morning and talk of our common problems . . . though I could never solve them! I am no great brain, just a neighbor and friend:

What I hope you will come to understand most from this book is that lots of women have all the problems you do. They have! I know, from my own experience, from what I hear, from what I read!

But even with all the problems, a housewife and home-maker multiplied is all that keeps America going.

Love is the greatest thing you have to give. Give it freely . . . yes, even if it is expressed through washing dishes and doing laundry. Never do "chores" if you are not in the mood. Wait till you want to do them because of what it will or can mean to someone else. That laundry and those weeds in the garden will wait for you and your right feeling about them.

Do what you can. But . . . enjoy it, if possible. Never sit and worry about what you have to do. If it bothers you that much, get up out of that chair and get it done. The dividends in "peace-of-mind" are worth the effort.

A pat on the back is what you need and I put that on this page: consider yourself patted, but good. Mrs. Homemaker, I think you are the most wonderful person on earth! You are the very backbone of family life.

Without your voluntary letters and sharing, this book could not have been written. I thank you from the bottom of my heart.

And I send my love,

Heloise

For Your Notes

Index

COLLECTION OF
COOK BOOKS

If your bookseller does not have these titles, you may order them by
sending retail price, plus 10¢ for postage and handling to: MAIL SERVICE
DEPT., Pocket Books, Inc., 1 West 39th Street, New York, New York 10018.
Enclose check or money order—not responsible for orders containing cash.